The Philosophical Hack:
The Concluding Unscientific Postscript to *Event*

THE PHILOSOPHICAL HACK

The Concluding Unscientific Postscript to Event

By Cedric Nathaniel

The First Part

O D   P A R C E L ~ 2 0 1 8

**The Philosophical Hack: The Concluding
Unscientific Postscript to Event**

The First Part. Copyright © 2018 by Lance A. Kair

First Printing: December 2018

ISBN 978-0-359-26580-0

OD PARCEL
Louisville. Colorado.

secondmusic.org

"Something happened to me that was outside my own plans. And after that I went where I was taken."

~Lancelot on returning from the Quest for the Holy Grail.

THE PHILOSOPHICAL HACK:
The Concluding Unscientific Postscript
to *Event*

The First Part

> "…I shall be telling this with a sigh
> Somewhere ages and ages hence…"
>
> *~Robert Frost.*

Robert Frost said his poem *"The Road Not Taken"* was a joke between himself and his friend Edward Thomas. Yet Thomas's students, to whom he then read the poem, took it very seriously[1]. Perhaps it may be said that all writing might be weighed in this manner. Of course, there are those in the humanities who would

---

[1] Katherine Robinson on poetryfoundation.org wrote the *poetry guide* for *"The Road Not Taken"*

argue their endeavors are not funny, have no comedic element, and perhaps the more analytical-scientific bent would think it humorous to say that theirs are neither, based as they are in a neutral logic. This essay grants the seriousness of philosophical proposals wherever needs be found, as they can be.

The foregoing essays are less partisan. One might say they are equally dramatic as comic. If the weight of tragedy is found in the coming together of reduction, the comedy is in the splitting apart that which must stay unified. This is a route of philosophy less taken; this is the speaking of what is supposed to remain silent, or that which is unspeakable[2]. No metaphysical structure will be built through the special privilege of reasoned thought; arguments here made are passive and for verification.

---

[2] Our attention is drawn to the relationship between *unknowable* and *unspeakable* through the 14th century piece of Christian mysticism called "*The Cloud of Unknowing*". The former supposes to indicate through inference the true nature of God by what lay beyond what is knowable, and the latter proposes the true nature of Being is found as the unknowable marks a condition of what is knowable.

Proposals are not drawn from any state of privilege but that of pleasure, *Jouissance*, in the sense that Roland Barthes gives us in the French: It is my pleasure to have read as it is my pleasure to write. I have found no position, but a position I have. The arguments will accrue and be discussed, but much the same as Frost, Barthes and, I will add poignantly, Ludwig Wittgenstein, at the end of argumentative positions few will have understood this essay. Most simply do have the pleasure of understanding their involvement with communication. With doubt some will know, and those can claim a legitimacy throughout the world, if not history, for the humor is stinging; like a funny bone, painful, yet bringing a laugh along with it. The seriousness of the sensation of smacking the elbow just right is accompanied by the persistent moment of disbelief that one could be so dense; one cannot but laugh at what comes to mind as the silliness of the whole event.

*

The meaning or substance of philosophy has been proposed in various ways, from problems and solutions, to critical thinking, to a way of living. Similar to Martin Heidegger's Dasein, or "Being-There", but without the contradicting definitional implication (only Being), *philosophy* for this essay is *that which is involved*; that which *is* not extricated from the situation. Hence, an outlier might task us to comprehend the last of the 20th century in mind of an effect of Wittgenstein's philosophical revelation: The manner by which human communication takes place has been uprooted, terms only reveal other terms, and these terms have no apparent necessary relation to other terms. Discourse is left without a ground and things without substance. How might we speak of this situation when the grounds for involvement have been suspended? In this single moment, near all the philosophy of the 20th century is indicted.

*

The Existentialist label of Kierkegaard and Nietzsche and their demanding condemnations aside, Wittgenstein can be viewed as the son of nihilism, but with Ludwig, all that we may know was lifted, suspended, even as we fell.

The aspirations of these philosophical prophets were absorbed in the failing, leaving any appeal to what is outside of knowing a move to invoke the chaotic and or nonsensical[3], and any appeal to what may be 'more than' merely a move which allows for the perpetual application of mundane 'same-ness'. Here we are stuck in the middle of two escape routes, two 'lines of flight', as it were, both which end up returning us to the 'regular' place. What might be outside of it is absurd, then an abyss, then chaos, and what might be more than it is more of just the same, infinite relative multiplicity. What are we to do?

As the 20th century fell into a pit of nothingness, it was filled with empty assertions of propriety grounded in the potential which human beings have to manipulate. The economics of Karl Marx began to take on new meaning. There was no escape from the nonsensical reasoning which could make a plausible argument out

---

[3] Some current philosophical trends have said just as much; for example, Graham Harman and Object Oriented Ontology (Object Oriented Philosophy), it seems, likes chaos.

of anything (out of nothing) so the remaining (ungrounded or self-grounded) situation must reflect relations and manipulations of power, and, because now the link between the term and the object had been fractured if not destroyed, the very idea of economy and politics were likewise problematized into oblivion. Only a rhetorician could suggest there was art in all the struggle, and nobility in the angst; only the artists could communicate the emptiness of Being launched into a space with no perception of gravity, and no direction home. In this environment, only a philosopher who makes no argument about Wittgenstein would dare suggest that such a temporal movement –a move of falling out of time – never took place; such an argument would become a fantasy of delusion.

Nihilism comes complete in the fact that a whole century of human activity still occurred, albeit, within nothing, from nowhere toward nothing. Still we are dealing with the fall out of such a blow, intensely set on coming up with a salve for that most depressing, insistent and somehow accelerating pain of existence.

Nonetheless, others have overcome the trauma and we are allowed to say that many philosophers do not understand their own proposals. Often enough we need others to understand outright what we could only notice and describe.

*

We might not improve on Mr. Frost's poem,

TWO roads diverged in a yellow wood,
And sorry I could not travel both
And be one traveler, long I stood
And looked down one as far as I could
To where it bent in the undergrowth;   5

Then took the other, as just as fair,
And having perhaps the better claim,
Because it was grassy and wanted wear;
Though as for that the passing there
Had worn them really about the same,   10

And both that morning equally lay
In leaves no step had trodden black.
Oh, I kept the first for another day!

Yet knowing how way leads on to way,
I doubted if I should ever come back.   *15*

I shall be telling this with a sigh
Somewhere ages and ages hence:
Two roads diverged in a wood, and I—
I took the one less traveled by,
And that has made all the difference.   *20*

but perhaps we could rewrite it, leave out
all the middle which can lead into
multitudinous interpretation, stay with
spirit in which it was written, and say

Two paths diverged in a melancholy wood,
And sorry I could not travel both
And be one traveler, long I stood
'till saw that I could;

Two roads diverged in a wood, and I –
I took one less traveled by,
And that is why all the difference.

This essay is about two routes.
The first is the route from which is
supposed all routes stem, and to which all
routes lead; we can call this The One Route,

because it is concerned with unity, philosophical reduction and commonality. We can call this One Route the metaphysical route, full of assertions and debates; as we might see, this is the *cosmological* route, the religious route, the route that philosophy wants to tell is ontological and having nothing to do with religion. The other route, which cannot have a proper name until we sit without becoming merely another route in the One Route, is the other route. Whatever route it is, this essay takes it; this essay concerns establishing a parameter to a thing which is understood to have no parameters. If it is a world of discourse, then we need be mindful to speak in a particular manner about things.

Latour

Bruno Latour begins his book, "*An Inquiry into Modes of Existence*", with an analogy of a path up a mountain to bring us into what he will describe as various modes of existence. These modes are characterized by what he calls a *pass*, each mode representing various ways Beings arrive at and pass over an unnoticed contradictory situation. While Latour conjures various labels for some 14 modes which divide up existence in an interesting manner, their particular descriptions are not our concern in this essay; only the primary notion of a *pass* is useful here. This essay handles what he indicates by the proposal of a *pass* and what must occur in order that he would need, or be able, to come up with the notion. A *pass* is a mechanism of existing which moves us over otherwise unpassable areas, such as a chasm or an abyss, and in the philosophical case, areas in knowledge that would contradict our ability to know we are existing. Latour posits various manners, modes, which accompany or can be associated with various existences, however, the very simple idea of a *pass* shows us that what is needed for philosophy is a way to speak about what has so far remained silent.

If indeed the Postmodern showed us what voices of the category[4] are Being left out of the discussion of the text, i.e. through the enforcement of binaries good/bad, right/wrong, civilized/primitive, colonizer/colonized, oppressor/oppressed, whiteness/people of color, sex/gender, etcetera, then a *pass* shows us what is Being left out of the category itself; in other words, what is involved in the category of the human being. The notions of post- and trans-human attempt to grapple with this finality, but Latour has given us theoretical frames by which various events can be told that were not able to be told without having other various disclaimers, such as 'fantasy', 'illusion', 'insanity' to name a few, attached to them. Philosophy has painted itself into a corner, so new methods are needed;

---

[4] What voices we could associate with an encompassing *meta-narrative*.

Latour has given us his bid. We thus move to turn philosophy on its head.

He begins his venture into the various modes through the example of a mountain trail. There, before us, is a scenic mountain and the beginning of the trail that will lead us to the wonderful view at the top. The trail, though, is not always clear and so someone has given us a map of the trail which has a rather crude drawing of the mountain, a line for the trail, landmarks drawn, symbols and various features that a hiker will encounter as they follow the path, to know they will not get lost and are proceeding correctly to make it to the vista. Latour has various names for the various kinds or configurations of passes, but one of the first *passes* he describes is the *pass* that allows us to see the mountain in the map and the map as the mountain. He notes that there is nothing which goes between the mountain and the path which attaches to the map itself, and the symbols on the map only very roughly appear similar to the landmarks they represent (the symbols are two dimensional, there is no scale on the map, only relative position, the map is barely 8 inches square and the mountain thousands of feet tall, for instance) and yet we can 'follow' the map and we will get to the actual destination on the mountain itself. He says that this is an example of a *pass*, as well then indicating a type of existence or manner of knowing existence; something passes over the inconsistencies of sense to allow the map and the mountain to come together to be things similar enough that we may join the two in a real experience of existence. This first and particular example of a *pass* does not necessarily translate its kind into the other types, but it does give an example of how at least the possibility of a *pass* can have credence.

Without going into the distinctive characteristics of all his modes attempting to discover which one I am enacting in this essay or making an argument for or against his model, I nevertheless have made, as I take now, an opening. Regardless of the judgment that will come down upon it, I am in a certain debt to Latour for noticing the need and making at least the attempt; more people will be open now to the possibility of being open, rather than just being open in general. Yet, we also notice his particular analogy appears to weigh in to an assumption of just where we are and where we might want to go...

The Philosophical Path

Remove, for a moment, your reader self from the modern and city life and imagine two towns. Actually, imagine that there are only these two towns. They trade with each other and co-exist with each other, are dependent upon one another. They are two distinct towns, so also imagine that they each have their own ways, their own fashion of dress, culture and in general of doing things, but they are nevertheless linked and similar; one could say that they are not as different from each other as the citizens of either town would think of the other. There is a huge wilderness between the towns that is traversed by a path. This path has been worn enough through the years to see it if you know what you are looking at and for, but also is often difficult to travel and you can get lost. The terrain is vast and the path splits off in various places going to streams and hillsides, lakes and meadows, giant trees, and all sorts of interesting wilderness sites. There is a network of paths that go to all these places and, if followed, will always lead to one of the towns, eventually and inevitably. Along these various paths one can see and get a pretty good layout from the various views around and upon the vast wilderness, as well as where each of the towns lay. Part of living in either town is a general education of the paths of wilderness (just stay on the path!), but also of knowing who to trust to know the way through the wilderness so you *don't* get lost.

At some point in the past there was only one town. The other town was part of myth and legend or even a religious kind of belief in the possibility of more. The other town was part of the wilderness then, of the great beyond, of infinite possibility and unknowing. Ages ago, a few brave and adventurous people went out to see what was out there. Many of them came back and reported upon various mysteries, various aspects of the wilderness and amazing sites, how to get there and back, but their maps and descriptions largely figurative and imprecise. Much time passed, and many such adventurers and their reports had to be made before anyone got a real sense of what was out there.

Eventually paths were developed; some that proved easy and more direct wore-in and remained, but many more were consumed by the brush and weather. One day the other town was discovered and a similar process of establishing a path between them went on. Over time, the wilderness came to be known by the retreading of the paths to the more notable and exciting sites, and became merely 'the forest', 'the jungle', 'the tundra', 'the desert', 'the mountains' and such, became known and then included with the paths which navigated between the towns, togehter became 'the world'. The wilderness itself, as an actual thing, disappeared to knowledge.

Discourse and a Brief History of Modern Philosophy

In our modern situation, what we generalize to call philosophy can be thought of as a path between two places, a starting place and an ending place. There was a time when we did not know what philosophy would produce or what it was addressing, but now all the paths have been made definite and been mapped, soon they will be paved, and massive amounts of consumer traffic will cross them. Philosophy in this analogy and as an extension of historical progress is defined by these paths and anyone who claims philosophy is inevitably lead onto the path toward the other town, and indeed encouraged to stray off of the paths. By now, everyone who would let them go wander knows that they will inevitably return to the path with reports of what the paths define by their cutting through the forests, the meadows, the deserts...

This is also to suggest that because all the paths have been found (even as they may not have been defined as such), if we are to speak of anything else then we must be also be speaking of the paths, following the way the paths show, gaining our bearings with reference to the paths. So; in philosophy, in the area where discourse is the final reduction[5], to say that "nothing exists outside of discourse" is just to say that we are speaking of an identity, namely, 'nothing = outside of discourse': The only possible way to get around this is to use discourse differently, which then regularly argues the original point.

We must answer this riddle before we go, if we are to go; else, anymore, we are living an anachronism, a perpetuation of the same as now. An argument that would propose that all the paths have been explored is evidencing what we can call a philosophy which is oriented upon objects in a certain manner.

*

---

[5] See below.

This aspect of existence, of orientations upon objects, might not be apparent to some readers. Rebuttals will arise; first against the notion that all philosophical paths have been traversed and second centering around a simple observation that discourse does not encompass all that exists, that there are other things besides discourse. The most persistent counter to both of these statements (all philosophical paths have been found and all is discourse) is that the individual has, or is otherwise privy to, a sort of personal space that is recognized often as 'mind' and is filled out by thoughts and feelings, sensations and moods, and various sorts of experience. In this situation, all the routes of philosophical speculation cannot possibly have been accounted for, and as well, given the variety of individual occurrences and experience, not to mention the motions of the planets and stars and the cellular activity of bacteria, as well as the infinity of all occurrences, discourse cannot contain all the possibility of existence. So, before we get to the description of the situation at hand, the situation we are faced with, the situation that bars any movement forward, we need to talk about discourse. We need to make the argument about why nothing exists outside of discourse. We will have to first come to certain conclusions in order to do so, as well to be able to travel the road of recent Western Philosophy without obstacles.

There are three arguments that can be made and one manner by which to get around the reduction of all things to discourse. The absolutely reliable manner is to deny the argument. This is the *weak* move of philosophical dealing with the issue, but it is nevertheless the most easy and effective: Deny it. By simply discounting it out of hand, discourse ceases to encompass all that can exist and we can talk about anything we want, some or all of which is not discursive. As we will get into with this essay, this manner is the usual way philosophy moves, by *passes*. For now, we must notice that philosophy as a general ideal thing or category, erects a vision of itself as wide open to possibility, and thus has a correspondingly firm methodology in place through which every possibility and instance of knowledge can be put to task.

We have already encountered two of the arguments. The first takes its cue (a *pass*) from the contradiction of Ludwig Wittgenstein (see below), a cue to move in a certain direction, along a certain vector of representation. This argument would say that discourse is a phenomenon of speech, involved with the brain, lungs and mouth specifically, but the whole body in general if we take into account what we know as 'body language'. This argument would then move to say that this particular manifestation of existence, i.e. discourse, has no more privilege to holding all existence than any of the parts that produce discourse. While this rebuttal does work, this essay also concerns the logistics of it working. For now, we yet see that in the effort and activity of making the counter proposal, it is using discourse to tell us how discourse is not containing all of existence; in short it is using the manner of denial. The second manner is really the same as the first and changes approach only in the way it categorizes existence. Here, while we might admit that discourse can be *used* to influence, create or otherwise manifest real existing things, there are things that exist outside of the field of discourse which nevertheless effect how discourse is used; this is a claim often heard by some recent Realist philosophers. Yet, this also simply denies that discourse has been recruited for the purpose of telling us about something that exists outside of discourse, but it plays sleight-of-hand by limiting 'discourse' to particular clausal organizational structures to say *the* discourse; for instance, the discourse of right-wing conservatives is outside of the discourse about bird migration.

The third argument is more subtle than the others because it relies less upon analytical logic. The thinker-of-thoughts, what we will term the "central thinker", is brought out for this rebuttal. This approach says that the *idea* of discourse can claim no more privilege than any other idea, at least no more than can be claimed through the established methodological criterion of logic. This rebuttal may appear to have the same basis as the others, yet it says something more than that to which the others attest; it raises the stakes of the argument. While the others rely upon an implicit common understanding of parties involved for consideration, this last argument *explicitly* tells us what parties *are* involved. Not only that, but we can infer from the timbre of this assumption that what it is telling us requires no justification, that the criterion of its assertion is supposed as self-evident *everywhere it will occur.*

What develops from this notice is a significance of Wittgenstein that is most often set aside or ignored, and through this, the significance of other philosophers thus also come to be seen in new relief. This is a fundamental shift in reckoning, for the third argument presents to us what we are up against with the figure of the modern human being in the world. With this final recursive default, we remain in the world of Emmanuel Kant where existence itself is simply an ideal emanation; discourse becomes another kind of ideal category, or categorical idea, or simply another object of thought, the same kind of object of which the universe itself is assumed in kind, as an object of thought. This essay will also address the subtlety of the prosaic and ubiquitous common sense from which it derives its force. The simple counter to this last offering is the same as the others: "And yet discourse was used…".

Questions must reside in the awareness of what is being withheld by the use of discourse, and whether what discourse references is being divulged in its truth, which is to say, 'in-itself'. By this view, philosophy, as a structure of progressive scaffolding where human beings can only be known though a privileged self-reflection upon negotiations of power with their common individual sort and its manifestations, becomes highlighted as a problem. Yet, recognition of this implicit and largely unspeakable narrative about an historically static ground of thought – thought which nevertheless develops through keeping itself out of the picture, all the while casting evidence of itself everywhere – allows philosophy to be an indicator of what human beings are *in-themselves*, as what they are doing, which is to say, as an object in the universe, rather than an unlocalizable process of continual argument over various iterations of clausal structures. This then is significant because through this opening we can move with confidence into topics such as systemic racism and addiction.

No argument exists, that we can know of (yet) which can argue outside of discourse, or function outside of its telling, so another issue of this essay is what is involved with this apparent selectivity of philosophy. Questions that become salient are, "What universe is philosophy giving us?"; "What is philosophy withholding from us?"; "For what purpose is philosophy complicit?"

*

Most modern philosophical discussions about Wittgenstein revolve around and never seem to encounter the reason why his ideas had such an impact. Less a matter of philosophical issues, to grasp this, to comprehend the impact as well as understand why or how it is given lip service while remaining unrecognized, one must actually encounter the issue that he uncovers. Much of the real modern critical method is based in avoiding encountering what is 'actual' and is founded in always questioning that term which might land itself in having to account for something besides more discourse. In fact, so indebted modern method is to

Wittgenstein's revelation, it finds itself – actually establishes itself –at the ground of completely misappropriating his texts; and this is so much the case that this simply stated observation will, in fact, likey be taken as blasphemy, accompanied with every sort of authorial defamation of character from being uneducated to, in the end, perhaps more personal and direct insults. Argument fails in this instance because the terms of the debt (to Wittgenstein through misappropriation) are so construed as to prevent itself from having to account for its own groundless method; there is no argument that can get past a view suspended in a threat of liquidation. We will explore this feature of our modern state also.

As it is, then, we must be able to say certain things that cannot be argued but are nevertheless evident. We must be allowed to describe the situation truly without a premature and derailing relativistic antagonistic rebuttal. Particularly, the impact of Wittgenstein's finding is not only the encounter with his findings, but an encounter with what is *not* impacted, or how the impact was diverted, *deflected* and basically avoided, through a situation of reason that was already present in the estimation of what reason is; history, lineage and tradition is leaned upon to create an antagonism which only exists within the establishment of its own defense.

*

The limits of Reason, as an institution, can be summed up in the statement "It is not reasonable for reason to have to defend itself against another reason". For this essay, this type of reason that cannot see beyond its own view, that insists its method of argument is able to successfully argue the primacy and sensibility of itself for all that is reasonable, rational and sensible, we call *conventional*. As well, the precipitate that is found once the Wittgenstein moment condenses in thought – out of the ether of ideas onto the ground of actual situation – and has impacted thought as to disrupt it, once the significant moment bares weight upon thought, the ubiquity that we call common that is left over from the contradiction therein, we associate with *conventional philosophy*. The result of the encounter with Wittgenstein's work actually functions to show a division in the Being of existence, a division in the estimation of what is already there for reason to work to be reason. It is no mere coincidence that the effort of Western Colonialization begins to become problematized at this moment in the early 20th century, for there becomes what we could call major and minor reasons that no longer answer to the hegemonic power of the majority to be deemed unreasonable, uneducated or ignorant. Yet Reason is upheld despite the fact that it cannot be proven to have reproduced itself in an image it cannot recognize. Hence, the reason that substantiates itself as an assailable common ground of thought, which then asserts *its* manner as *the omnipresent* manner of Being, at one time called *ideology,* as a kind of systemic enforcement of 'idealized' power, now evidences itself in an argumentatively more honest frame as a feature or tenant of a *faith.*

   A key item in the appropriation of a divergent *reason* is an acknowledgement that before Wittgenstein, Descartes could be said to be the witnessing of the self-evidence of thought; philosophy did not orient itself upon particular phenomenon but rather phenomena was taken to be complicit with Reason[6]. Before Kant was the working of reason for the world. After Kant was the self-*reflective* reason of the world. This consolidation thus was defined reflexively with reference to what was thereby obviously variegated and inconsistent across the human situation. Hence, we understand the issue that Kant treated is the difference that arises between superstition and reason; the result as well as the motivating force for the next +/-200 years of philosophy, is staked within the self-reflecting claim of personal inspiration through communion with 'other', together comprising the whole world, the claim of which conceptual defaults were well worked out by Georg Hegel. Reason developed itself with reference to civilization and apparent domination of the rest of the world as a matter of course.

---

[6] *Cogito, ergo sum.* The Cartesian world is thus defined by not reflecting further upon this situation; I am thinking, and the extension of thought past itself is thereby the evidence of the scientific object.

Though one could say that Soren Kierkegaard's despair and Fredrich Nietzsche's angst were already evidencing the soon collapse, Wittgenstein's fact was the collapse of the unproblematized self-reflecting identity. Once we can understand what this actually means, what it actually *does*, what actually occurs due to the rupture of the reasonable link between thought and thing, then we can likewise understand how philosophy after the collapse began to operate under a certain form of *intentional dishonesty*, and this is to indicate an intentional institutionalization of dishonesty in Being, which is to say, as an impositional effort toward a propriety of thinking, a proper manner to have reality. Though there is plenty (way too much) to say about this situation, the tracing of this dishonesty runs through Martin Heidegger's thought in his "destitute" spirit, as well as Theodore Adorno's "negative dialectics", to name only two authors attempting to find a way to confront what we could call the categorical imperative of dishonesty. Jean-Paul Sartre can be seen to represent a first divestiture from this indoctrination of intension[7] by placing existence before essence, pointing out this change just indicated above, and 'rewinds the clock' in the attempt to confront what went wrong. By invoking Kierkegaard as the first Existentialist he beckons philosophy to reconsider what Soren could have meant by the "contemporary"[8]. Yet, the irony that was perpetuated, the winding down of an unreasonable and uncontrollable duplicity of thought, was unable to break free from the imposition of dishonesty necessitated by the disruption of, what had up till the early 20th century was, the common world of Being.

---

[7] The terms *intension* and *intention* is another word play that supposes to be able to locate more specifically the truth of the situation at hand. Simply put, the former is the capacity of word or language use, and the latter is the potential of activity. One might think of *intension* as a compound word, 'in-tension' because any term holds within itself a tension which is the difference between the idea and the symbol of the word. In this essay, though, I use the spelling *intension* to pronounce the tension involved in the presented clause, wherever is may occur, but also so not to exclude the usual spelling *intention* and its regular meaning.

[8] See Kierkegaard's *"Philosophical Crumbs"*

What I am calling 'dishonesty' might be summarized in the context of Jose Ortega y Gasset[9]. Early in his book, *"What Is Philosophy"*, he speaks of "...two worlds, antagonistic in composition..." which exist in necessary relation with time; temporal and atemporal, reality and truth, respectively. This antagonism, though, to use Ortega y Gasset as relief, cannot be said to exist essentially were it not for some sort of interlocutor, some middle ground which notices this antagonism. This middle ground he calls "thought", and he frames thus the three situations noted since ancient times; namely, the eternal and atemporal truth, the temporal reality of things and negotiation, and the point where the two worlds come together, thought.

Here we have the example of what is dishonest in the context of history. To

---

[9] Zizek uses the notion of 'naivety' to indicate a manner of separating types of knowing for the purpose of speaking about *particular* circumstances. I use the term 'dishonesty' in a manner referring to knowledge itself and what is *universal* as a situation. These approaches are not exclusive as much as they are complimentary. We will discuss this facet of philosophy in a later part.

address this oddity, then[10], we have posited two routes and a particular manner by which we must speak if we are to proceed within an effort to communicate. What is dishonest is only in reference to the substance of statements that cannot, by definition, be included in the temporal negotiation. To be honest we would be perpetually giving and taking back in order to make any statement about anything, and any simple idea would take volumes to convey, never minding the convoluted manner that such a simple idea would have to take form to convey the totality of its implications. What occurs after Wittgenstein is a blatant revealing of two routes into philosophy. One denies or ignores the meaning the contradiction would impose upon sense for the sake of the underlying ideal of commonality; for example, with Ortega y Gasset using *thought*. The other one, then, perpetually attempts to include the contradiction in the discourse itself, accounting for the collapse of cosmological unity within the description of what is occurring. The dishonesty here is taken back through what we know as the

---

[10] It is odd that we would argue with him.

founding term[11], in this case 'thought', upon which such a discourse may proceed. In itself, in an assumed common arena of meaning, though, such a proposal is not dishonest; only through the notice, acknowledgment and the 'bringing into play' of the founding term, can we find situations that can be dishonest[12].

The distinction is not one that can be proven; where what is true must be

---

[11] A *founding* or *foundational term* is a term within a clausal structure which serves to ground the phrase in a larger context that is unidentified; i.e. that which is given for the meaning of the argument or presentation. For our example here of Ortega y Gasset, 'thought' is a founding term because it is the one idea (term) which is given-to-be-assumed in order for the rest of the argument to have sense. Arguments are established in founding terms, but as well every instance of communication. Indeed the "phrase universe" of Lyotard concerns the founding term. I often refer to this term as the term which breaks through the façade of discursive reality. This will be discussed in a later Part.

[12] Being is that which is concerned with Being. In this concern, the instance of the founding term shows what is dishonest. This is not a metaphysical proposal because it says nothing about what continues outside of the situation.

proven, we have the indication of a common sort. Thus, to be honest, we can no longer be speaking within a certain common communicative domain. Honesty, in this respect, cannot have very much to do with the fact that dishonesty must be included in the manner by which we attempt to frame particular discourses in defined founded scaffoldings. We thus have the outline of two manners of coming upon things.

The Wilderness

The adventurer starts on the path but then disappears. She has not wandered off the path in expectation to find it again, but indeed has left the path. The possibility of this situation must lie in the fact that the paths have defined what the whole world is. According to the way one is supposed and assumed to go, there is *nothing* that does not occur with reference to the path: There is nothing outside of the world because we have mapped, or have drawn plans in mind of the map, for everything in the world; the paths define what the world is.

If this is the case, then we already know that the statement is not true. The adventurer does not find 'interesting' overlooks or beautiful vistas that link back to exciting experiences that everyone can talk about and relate with. The adventurer finds herself 'gone', 'off the map', atop mountains, in valleys, wading streams, laying in meadows, stalking dunes, and not in *the* mountains, *the* valleys, etcetera.

Each of these wild events speak of themselves and yet communicate the wilderness that actually fills in the world beyond the paths. These places do not communicate the world; the world is communicated with reference to the path, but thus along the path. In the wilderness, one does not go here to there; rather, one travels, looks, experiences and describes. Where along the path, one may have 'had a great time' or has opinions about why this spot is preferable to that place, how the view from this ledge represents the valley more accurately than the one from the hillside, in the wilderness the whole of the terrain is visible from the events in themselves communicating the wilderness that it is. When one speaks of the stream, she speaks of the mountains and the trees because as she travels in the wilderness, trees or sand, or brush or tundra are everywhere, and streams all over and mountains. At each place, she has a view and can speak about all the places in different ways yet while telling of the same place, the wilderness. From the stream, mountains jut out in to sky; from treetops, streams wiggle in and out of existence; from mountains, a stream is a black line which carves out a forest. Everywhere one goes in the wilderness she can describe the particular stone in many ways in many instances and still be talking about the same stone. The stream trickling down the mountainside from its origins, is the same stream described as a raging torrent of water crashing upon the rocks. A common language is used but somehow communicates something specific in one instance and something different in another without communicating a multiplicity of things. There is not 'this stream' and 'that river' as though they actually are different things; there is not 'the green tree' at noon and then another, separate tree called 'the black tree' at midnight. In the wilderness we are able to describe the same objects, the same situations from various vantage points, various environments, and different moments[13]. Along the path, by contrast, one can only speak of individual things which exist in the common world which may or

---

[13] A parallax view. The typical postmodern subject is concerned with the individual real semantic expressions of political identity; parallax as *representing* real content. A parallax view as a *description* of the situation concerns only two orientations upon objects.

may not have a multiple of meanings in various contexts; the ontology of real things is determined by the meaning which takes place in the common ideal of thought. Common people can choose which meaning has meaning, that is, so long as the creation of 'meaning' is a non-negotiated reality of being human[14].

---

[14] In mind of The Two Routes, we are not to read 'common people' as an exceptional argumentative position; which is to say, a description of the common person does not represent that the author or the reader is not supposed common.

Postmodern

Once the Postmodern arrives, we have the last remaining credible attempts at breaking the cycle of institutional dishonesty. The 'horsemen' of the Postmodern, the short, short list, are Jacques Derrida, Guiles Deleuze and Felix Guattari, and Jean-Francois Lyotard. The combination of their efforts brings good light upon the degrading issue of philosophy by their individual attempts at reconciling what had reached such a discrepant state. The significance of their reconciliations are only recognized under certain conditions, and we thus are involved in describing the conditions, rather than making an argument about various subsequent details. Three conditions can be used to show how their reconciliations are perpetually avoided for the sake of the common; the stakes of reconciliation are the topic of this essay.

Deleuze and Guattari

After Heidegger, we can see a philosopher who proposes the truth of the situation honestly in Guiles Deleuze[15]. Mind that we are looking through a particular lens, focused wide but clear; we see that his is one of a most successful attempt – I would argue the best[16] – that anyone can do in the giving-and-taking away that would be required for a truthful communication of the situation at hand of, what we could call, 'actual' existence, the 'common' existence of everyday living of making beds, mowing lawns and drinking beers, i.e. of Being as it can be involved with everyday situations. I call his discussions 'poetic-prose' because his works while rigorous in a prosaic sense, also require a certain poetic attitude in order to understand. This is because one must not only be able to follow the assemblage of senses and propositions, but also be able to

---

[15] Going forward, I reference the collaborations of Deleuze and Guattari through using Deleuze.

[16] Francois Laruelle does not give and then take away, as we will see. Rather, Laruelle does the best at giving it all back by taking it all away.

suspend the idea that is being conveyed to see that they are, in effect, nullifying the initial meaning[17]. The meaning of the logical string of sense which indicates various aspects of reality and applying that meaning to its object, contradicts that the string is talking about something other than the string itself; it is giving while taking away. Indeed, Deleuze considered himself a metaphysician.

*

We are not here to put forth an argument about what Deleuze might have been saying and if it makes sense or has

---

[17] I am of course speaking about his metaphysical ontology and not the consequences which follow of the order. His subsequent discourses, or discourses of subsequence, his more political discussions, are in effect religious followings of a cohesive Being, the extrapolation of the metaphysics into the 'everyday' occurrences of reality. His metaphysical ontology derives its total appearance through the balanced giving and immediate taking away, as I will discuss. As a side note; Nick Land, as a sort of Deleuzian fanatic, takes everything away and, literally, gives nothing back. Land is a philosophically religious fundamentalist in the worst sense.

any value as a truth regime, though. The argued meaning of his works are incidental in as much as this essay is a description of what is not incidental about what he is saying. The argument is the description; this is not a conventional argument constructed of premises and theorems. We ask the reader to suspend her dependency upon the established philosophical lineages and protocols and open herself up to the possibility that the supposed lineage of ideas will nevertheless be expressed in this essay; we ask for the philosopher to come forward, ahead of theoretician and rhetorician. I ask: While a person may study ideas in order to frame how and what they might think, did she learn philosophy through first considering what other authors had to say to *then* come to her own opinion?

*

Two 'platforms' of Deleuze interests us; the *rhizome* and the *plateau*. Again, quickly, we ask the rebuttal and commentaries to wait till the end of the essay; there is no wrong in what is able to be done, only in what is not admitted of limitations. What is wrong is when we overestimate sense and then demand its truth in the same motion. Much of philosophy works through a systematic-logical-analytical method of presenting the structure of argument. Both philosophical schools (analytical and continental, below) do this; they keep to the path, discussing philosophical things and their speculations with reference to a usual methodological line of Reason, a particular manner of presentation and appropriation, a 'rule book' of how to do philosophy, by which ideas may be said to be able to be questioned. In this manner of philosophical knowledge all the debates are studied for the purpose of having the next debate to see just how much information has been uploaded successfully, to see if a different juice just might come out of the orange this time. It is a standardized and recognized valid method, upon an *un-argued* given of the common.

While still speaking in a particular manner[18], the argument that Deleuze

---

[18] We have already noted that in order to convey the truth of the situation we must speak in a certain

presents, on the other hand, fractures itself as well as most conventional efforts that wish to break into it; it is not linear. It cannot be contained within confines of a particular path because it continually disrupts the path, or as Deleuze himself might say, his discourse deterritorializes its own territory. This is what I mean by bringing the contradiction as contradiction into the discussion of the idea that relies upon as it rejects the contradicting element. He attempts to remain true to what has *occurred* in the context of philosophy, as I have spoken about Wittgenstein; philosophers of this type are not obsessively concerned about making an argument *about* what the philosophical tradition puts forth. Deleuze thus grants us a 'view from below' or what could be called an *underdetermined* manner, as well as from above, or *overdetermined* manner[19], and thus

---

manner. This is to say, that the manner must be noted, and in this notice is not meant to be heard in the normalized and regular conventional timbre: It must be noted that we are speaking in a certain manner.

[19] Graham Harman also uses these notions in his *Object Oriented Philosophy*, which have some association here.

presents a picture of reality that is quite compelling if not difficult to argue against.

rhizome

The *rhizome* is an analogy 'from below' of the subject encounter with the world. It is overdetermined in the sense of dishonesty noted above (that the term identifies a specific and static thing[20]), and it is underdetermined for meaning in the manner that it approaches the situation. He did not make up the term but instead uses a term already defined in the attempt to show a philosophical picture. A standard, not philosophical, definition of *rhizome*

> *"...is a modified subterranean stem of a plant that sends out roots and shoots from its*

---

[20] A *static* thing refers to the apparent thing at hand. For instance, a cup sitting on the table next to me is *static* because it remains a cup every time I am thirsty, as well when I knock it over because I am clumsy. Mind that this is a description of what occurs and not a metaphysical proposal nor an ontological argument.

nodes. Rhizomes are also called creeping rootstalks and rootstocks. Rhizomes develop from axillary buds and grow horizontally. The rhizome also retains the ability to allow new shoots to grow upwards."[21]

Deleuze uses this analogy to describe how subjectivity (but its ontological presence in general) appears in the world or as world, as the case may be. In short, the world, as subjectivity can be inscribed in the knowing of world, appears as the shoots, as individual subjects and objects, while 'underneath' it is all connected. A characteristic of a rhizome is its resiliency, an ability to defy destruction; from the surface above ground, shoots can be destroyed but the plant itself (under the surface) does not die, but then will send up shoots in other places. To the view above ground appears a multitude of things, and 'in reality' we address these various things as though they are 'in-itself' subjects and objects that are affected individually and

[21] https://en.wikipedia.org/wiki/Rhizome

essentially by physical, mental and communicative sense.

There are many ways of viewing this idea, and he gives us a few manners by which to make sense of it and its implications. The idea of a central thinker or mind which lay underneath its overt expressions that appear in the world is one simple way to use the analogy. But in another fashion, he is speaking of what the subject (-world-object) does: It defies locality[22] . Like a magic trick or even a hydra with many heads that sprout new ones when others are chopped off, the subject (-world: rhizome-shoot) is not localizable – and this is key – *like other human individuals*. This is to say that the various descriptions that Deleuze gives of the functioning and application of the rhizome analogy grant us something through one view, when looking at it in one way, and gives us something entirely *different* when viewed from another angle. This other way defies locality, specificity, and the finitude that identifies individual human beings *in* the world. In

---

[22] We recall Graham Harman's "real objects withdraw from experience".

other words, when we consider the rhizome idea along with other ideas of his, such as "deterritorialization" and "body without organs", he at once is giving something and then taking it away. His discourses present the reader to a situation whereby the existential quality of knowledge itself is at issue; indeed, the existence of knowledge itself comes into question.

This materializes around whether he was speaking of something common, such as an individual thinking subject that every human being might be, or whether he is speaking of an exceptional, non-localizable situation that is uncommon, that is, not immediately knowable by everyone who reads and comes to understand what he is saying[23]. Either he is speaking about the common human individual (the subject and "subject of...") who is able to understand his discourses through the traditional methodological lineage of philosophical reason, or he is speaking

---

[23] This does not necessarily break down along lines of intelligence or education. Intelligence and education is assumed, whatever meaning we have for it.

about an uncommon situation that adjusts and responds naturally to confronting situations, appearing in different ways depending upon the situation at hand. If the case is the former, then we have nothing significant about philosophy but that at any moment some event can occur. If the case is the latter, though, then at each juncture the move responds in kind to the occasion, yielding things that appear as indeed different things, saying different things, using various terms and arrangements of terms, producing coherencies to each individual event of query, making different arguments about specific localizations, specific conceptual or linguistic territories. The subject-world here, then, merely says the same thing over and over *through* the different clausal structures, different 'shoots', *meaning* all the while the same non-local, rhizomic situation. What is common, or of the former, is that the various clausal presentations appearing 'above ground' are taken in their different forms to be communicating specific items to be grasped, 'ideal things' that are assumed to be indicating a number of various individual things and arguments about various specific things, abstract and concrete, true and false. What is rhizomic here, also, nevertheless always means and refers to the constancy of what is being withheld 'underneath' unseen and unacknowledged, or sometimes just plain denied by the conventional sort.

*

These are two basic 'instructions' for Being involved with Deleuze's ideas, and they cannot, in all honesty, be conflated or reduced to either to say that one is more true or more accurately tells us what he is meaning, because to do so necessarily assumes that he is speaking ironically and not directly. For example, it is not proper to say the term "deterritorialization" would *actually* be referring to an analogy due to the fact that using an argument about Deleuze's "deterritorialization" defies that the term had any actual meaning: In the act of using his arguments to make a further argument, the territory that "deterritorialization" occupies is relied upon[24]

---

[24] Ontological arguments are subjective assertions of actuality based in an inherent assumption that logic is denoting or dictating what is actually true of the

. The 'non-local' meaning, the one that gives as it takes back, the one that contains the collapse which is the Wittgenstein moment, just as the collapse is ignored, likewise is Deleuze's subject Being excluded from 'actual' philosophical possibility. This is the short-short synopsis of his metaphysics of Being. Some informed philosophers will charge this explanation as over simplified and thus incorrect but if there are subtleties or complexities that are being left out or missed here, then they are important only for the subsequent commentary or as they may appear elsewhere in this essay in different forms.

plateau

---

situation. As we see, because there is no ground for discourse, this kind of approach is ironic because it stems from and assumption of commonality, which, if we account for disagreement, is not being communicated. If we make an argument about, say, Deleuze's "deterritorialization" we therefore are assuming a direct communication where only an ironic one is actually occurring.

Deleuze's concepts are not necessarily to be understood as reducible to any other. However, each supports the other and describes the other; each being a particular view, a particular *parallax view*, upon the object of Being. This is the concept of the *plateau*. From each, every other can be viewed and described differently, and this difference then inscribes as it describes the *plateau*, yet while speaking from it. For this essay, the *plateau* adds to the metaphysical dimension of Being by explaining the manner by which the *rhizome* then may be spoken about and explained. A kind of map, or primer by which to interpret what is said, the *plateau* describes how the picture is being presented and the manner by which the Being should appropriate the *description* of rhizomic Being, just as the *rhizome* describes the Being of the *plateau*. Where a localization may appear, a territory of the *plateau*, for example, it is to be discerned from the 'line-of-reasoning', for a term, distinguished from the territory that is understood as occupied by reason. It sounds contradictory, but it is; the territory of the *plateau* with reference to the line-of-reason is to be understood as a *de-stabilization*, even while the *plateau* is stable in its regard to being that which destabilizes the line-of-reason. It is a giving and a taking away.

The conventional line-of-reason relies upon step by step premises that fall into theorems, which then gather together to make a proposal of proof, and this gathering is then understood to be the *necessary manner* by which the world manifests[25]. We find this format in the early philosophers, as a common effort, as well as ubiquitous to what we generalize now as the *analytical* school of philosophy; this method defines by its real presence a divergence in method against what is common by its very requirement for Being. The *plateau*, as a term for a divergent method, assumes an intact proof, a proof that is already known. What we have termed the "conventional method" will (as course) move to draw out the repercussions

---

[25] Metaphysics is a proposal of what is actually true. Whether or not the proposal admits that it is but one opinion among many does nothing to negate that it expresses as it inhabits an intension of the philosopher. It is ridiculous to entertain an ideal where someone would make a proposal that they didn't think represents veracity.

of having a proof intact before the argument is presented, and therefore cannot recognize this kind of proof. The problem lays out: First, such a divergent argument is thus working backwards and so is not really an argument at all, and second, that a proof that is already intact is what we in philosophy already call "*given*", and the method tells us that what is given for the argument must be laid out in the premises. In other words, we have a plausible explanation of why philosophers such as Ludwig's mentor, Bertrand Russel, had a hard-enough time with some manners of argument such that he (and others before him) began to refer to this different manner as the "continental" school.

Deleuze refers to this 'different' method in the title of his book "*A Thousand Plateaus*". The implication is that the method by which this philosophical situation is to be understood is not the same as the conventional method. A *plateau* can be used as a vantage point among many possible points of view. A certain simplistic conventional interpretation of this idea indicates, again, a localized individual human subject thinker who has a point of view, or subjective view or opinion upon things amidst a multitude of individuals who look out upon the world from their "*plateau*". Yet in the context of the rhizomic subject-world, with the *plateau* we have a different description of the same situation that the *rhizome* concept describes, yet through different terms. From the *plateau* a view is granted which overlooks the *entire* situation *because* it is given, already proven, already occurring. In this condition, the subject exits at all points (-world) but only at the moments that are given to a situation in and as a response. The *plateau* is thus that point which encounters or otherwise becomes a localized event; when something is spoken, to say something, only a particular set of terms will accurately describe or respond truthfully to the situation at hand. The *nature* of such an event thus destabilizes that situation of the localized subject due to the contradictory juncture through which such an encounter occurs. These two concepts, the *rhizome* and the *plateau* work together and function interchangeably, yet each describes the philosophical situation of Being from its own manner, its own Being, from its own *plateau*, if you will. One describes how the subject functions to show itself upon various occasions, and the other, how the subject is to be viewed in light of what it shows in its viewing, to show what it is: A de-ontological, non-local situation.

Derrida

Each of our three Postmodern authors grant manners of approaching the situation of this essay. While Deleuze comes closest to granting us a total metaphysical situation of Being in the manner that we usually think when we want to think about Being, Derrida takes a tack which speaks to what a subject *does first*, as opposed to what *it is*. These Postmoderns continued with Wittgenstein's shift as an inescapable condition, rather than merely another case of his own explanation, and attempted to further bring out the repercussions of it apparently not being actualized, or not being recognized as the paramount condition, through the concept of *difference*. What Deleuze may have emphasized in a strange and arguably eccentric manner, Derrida celebrates openly.

text and spirit

This open celebration[26] pairs well with his approach. The issue of discourse becomes pronounced and problematized with the issue of the text; again, a giving and a taking away. The question that he brings is less upon ontology, or Being as such, than its mechanisms; the mechanism by which any Being is possible. This mechanism is the knowing that comes only through the text.

What he means by text is everything that has to do with knowing. Upon entering this domain, oddly enough,

[26] Derrida is known for coining a play on the meaning of "difference" with the spelling (in French) "differance". The intentional misspelling is meant to encourage a shift, as I say, away from the common, yet as well, back into the common. To paraphrase: The meaning "to *dif*-fer" and "to dif-*fer*" create a contradictory state of being in the consideration of the term: to "be" different, is to thus "concede" the point, i.e. to give up in the (conventional) manner of thinking about difference, and come upon, as later Alain Badiou will coin, difference as indeed different. A giving and a taking, a removing and resettling.

we again find two manners of appropriating the text. The first question that should arise is whether there is a thought independent of text; is there a thought *upon* the text? In answering this honestly, we again come upon a contradiction. Similar to the way the Deleuze elaborates upon how Being can appear in two ways, Derrida is involved with the contradiction through the question of *thought*; the answer to the question "If anything exists outside of discourse (the text), then what is it?" is operative. Note that it is *the answer* which informs the reader of the text to what Derrida is saying: While there may be infinite configurations of answers, there is only two types of answers. In this essay I refer to this phenomenon as evidence of one's *orientation upon objects.* The answer, located as a question, evidences orientation. The answer, which is referred to in the adjective clause "always-already", either arises as the text is understood to be an object that thought reflects *upon,* or, as text itself the discourse that is used, 'thought' being another text.

The contradiction which arises to offend should be obvious: How can thought be inseparable from text? As well, we might then see, how philosophy before the modern era (but still and always) spoke of contradiction as the indicator of the direction to which the thought should lean; that is, it should move *away* from what is negated of the thought, or, the axiomatic rejection of what is *false*. Before the modern era, contradiction in philosophy was regularly and automatically formulated as a common-sense aspect of reasoning and amounted to the impassable limit by which reason was able to be formulated[27]; reason

---

[27] Reason is still formulated in this manner, but philosophy responded *only* to this manner before modernity. This essay uses the notion of a *conventional philosophy* as a response. As we will discuss later in this essay, we have evidence of a pre-modern philosophical ideal; it failed the ancient Greeks only to have Christianity solve the ontological problem of the apparent hole in reason. Indeed, Christianity is the solution to the ontological problem, but it is only a *true* solution in as much as there is *only* two possibilities involved with the singular potence and omnipresense of Reason, or as the Greeks might have called it, the *logos.* Modernity might be said to be the return of the religion of the *logos* under a different name; it has returned because the failure of reason has been forgotten.

itself could not be investigated because of the contradiction involved in having reason form reasonable ideas about how reason might exist[28].

The modern era can be characterized by a necessity to assert the historical truth as universal truth; in its conception, the modern era is also, ironically, the rising to awareness the problem of *reason*. The faculty of reason was understood to be a natural and inherently progressive feature in the course of human development, the latest manifestation of this progress, the move from a given common 'reason' into an aware 'Reason', was opposed to such implicated lesser human beings' reasoning as 'vulgar'[29] and

---

[28] In effect, honesty was what prevented an investigation in reason. Indeed; Being itself was thought to be impenetrable before Heidegger. Hence, the introduction to *post*-modernity in the early 20th century. The issues that arise in these kinds of projects of reason thus bring us to our day where humanity is more properly understood as a process, rather than an identity; as I say, a "universal object". Hence, the call for this essay.

[29] The Online Etymology Dictionary has this entry for "vulgar": late 14c., "common, ordinary," from

'superstitious'[30]. It was Kant who opened the door to investigating Reason by asking what it does, rather than what it is, by inducing the birth of knowledge rather than continuing to produce it, which is to say, to replicate it[31].

By this move, Kant's essay about *Pure Reason,* a crack in the façade of progressive unity was made, even while he could not witness it. The crack appears due to the problem that never seems to be asked: How could Reason be able to witness

---

Latin *vulgaris, volgaris* "of or pertaining to the common people, common, vulgar, low, mean," from *vulgus* "the common people, multitude, crowd, throng," perhaps from a PIE root **wel-* "to crowd, throng" (source also of Sanskrit *vargah* "division, group," Greek *eilein* "to press, throng," Middle Breton *gwal'ch* "abundance," Welsh *gwala* "sufficiency, enough") [not in Watkins]. Meaning "coarse, low, ill-bred" is first recorded 1640s, probably from earlier use (with reference to people) with meaning "belonging to the ordinary class" (1530). Related: *Vulgarly.*

[30] Kant's *"The Critique of Pure Reason"* indicts superstition.

[31] There is a critique of Marx somewhere in this notion.

what it does? If the focus of previous philosophers was around the (use-) Being of Reason, which yielded, as Kant says,

"... confusion and contradictions, from which it conjectures the presence of latent errors, which, however, it is unable to discover, because the principles it employs, transcending the limits of experience, cannot be tested by that criterion"[32],

then how was asking what it does any different? If we cannot know what it is, then how can we determine what effects are due to it? We can only speculate, so we should notice that this philosophical notion is a result of a conceptual default to a unitive human ideal that is given as it is assumed. It is this kind of self-reflecting justification which evidences a distinction of what has been missed by rejecting (or *passing* over) contradiction (that a common

[32] Emmanuel Kant. Preface to the 1781 first edition of *"The Critique of Pure Reason"*

humanity is an ideal form), which is to say, from what actively includes the contradiction in its deliberations. Because the collapse of the rift[33] that began with Kant could not be noticed by him, we can say that when Kant proposed his *Critique* he saw reality as involved in the understanding of the common (as he was a part of the common, although unequal in education and reasoning) progressing humanity, but also, was arguing from a situation that is already proven, already *given,* in the presentation of the discourse. While the *Critique* is available to be viewed as an argument about various localities, such as, *analytical* and *synthetical* knowledge, and *a posteriori* and *a priori* judgements, once a particular judgement has been made as to what is occurring in the text (-world), it is no longer possible to not see it as an argument about the *faculty*

---

[33] "The collapse of the rift" is the beginning of the elaboration of the *pass* which de facto is conventional thought unaware (in denial) of the rift. This particular contradiction is brought to a halt with Wittgenstein but is then passed over again to bring us to this Hack. Kant did not know that his proposal *could* be missed; this is then a kind of historical mark which ironically "begins the count" (Badiou) of a divergent reason.

of Reason that everyone (the common humanity) has access to individually or separately.

We can begin to understand the contradiction at play here and how it is incorporated into the *Critique* when we place our judgement in the context of Kant's program under the heading of *a priori* and *a posteriori*[34]: If an *argument* is being made, then the judgement itself about that argument is an *a posteriori* judgement, and analytical (according to causal agreement) at that. In other words, if we are to appropriate Kant's *Critique* as an argument to be considered, then we are using

---

[34] The traditional manner in which the expressions *a priori* and *a posteriori* are defined is in reference to the distinction between thought in consideration of experience of things in the world, that are usually called 'objects', and thought in consideration of things that are of a pure mental process. Thus, we have judgments that occur "prior", outside, or apart from direct experience with an object, and judgements that occur "after", behind or because of a direct encounter with a worldly object. *The Critique* concerns this former kind of judgement and knowledge, what he calls the *synthetical a priori.* see note (k)

experience to form a judgment, but if the point of Kant's thesis is the divulging of how the Pure Reason functions, then to assess his work *through* experience (of reading *the Critique*) is missing the point of his essay. For how could a person consider what is going on *a priori* while they are assessing that situation through the experience of reading a text about it, *a posteriori*?

The confusion that arises from this simple, yet incomplete, consideration of what Kant presents to us, accounts for the majority of philosophical proposals (as they might involve or reference Kant) for the next 200 years, and beyond; it frames what we are noticing as the problem of enlightenment. So, it is likewise philosophically improper to suspend the judgement *again* (to use the understanding of *experience* merely in order to make an argument about our position, which is to say, as a founding term) to discount what enlightenment is as it does; it is then as we say: It is indeed possible and valid –and indeed *present* – to view Kant along those conventional lines of reason. However, when we consider that his proposals stem from a proof that already exists, a subject that already has access to the whole of the situation, then we begin to understand why the issue is the *text* (but now more so the *term*) and not so much the faculty of reason or even thought and how they might work in individual people to develop arguments that may be considered and contested. This is because if the reason is pure, then there is no question as to what is occurring[35]; the resultant discourse is thus a description of what is already there, *prior to the experience of worldly things.*

*

[35] This is the meaning of the *categorical imperative.* It is a category that cannot be (or thus behave) in any manner other than what the category dictates (* the conflation of the categorical imperative across the unitive category of the human being brings the ethical judgment of *should*, i.e. a practical or hypothetical move where the categorical imperative implies a *should* or *ought,* and likewise introduces the irony of this 'transitional philosophy' which Kierkegaard so wittingly addresses through his philosophical-religious tropes). In this case, a Pure Reason cannot but occur in its purity of reason, consistent with itself, a reason that no argument can affect because the reason, by virtue of it being pure, has already answered the rebuttal –like a rhizome.

But this is not an essay about Kant. The point to be understood about Derrida comes to light when we see that he does not so much center his proposals around thought than around *spirit*. This move pronounces the distinction between discussion that uses discursive examples to talk about how knowledge may be structured[36], and text. The central issue of

---

[36] (k) Kant uses a discursive example to talk about how knowledge functions and makes a distinction in types of knowledge and the functions that occur due to the semantic restraint involved with each coupling. With *Analytical* statements, the predicate is part of the subject, such as "mammals have hair", because having hair is part of the definition of being a mammal. *Synthetical* propositions do not contain the subject in the predicate and need an outside verification for its truth value; "Books are entertaining" is synthetical because not all books are entertaining, so we have to find out about *this* book. Experience, in Kantian terms, is opposed to what could be called "the experience of thinking", or, reason. Kant does first grant that, in general, experience must always precede thought or reason, but he also recognizes once that occurs we are left with the situation where reason itself cannot be breached. He thus supposes that we can infer the nature or Being of reason itself through analyzing

the text is this distinction, for it indicates
the main problem that is never being

---

judgements, effects or evidence of reason, based in
experience of things or thought itself working in its
own space with logic.

The end run of this effort concerns
synthetical a priori judgements, ideas that arise
independent of experience based solely on the
workings of mind with logic. The usual manner of
appropriating his work is to conflate his analogy with
the thing in-itself, as though he is speaking of an
actual thing or situation called Reason, its Being
reflecting itself into its effects, into the discursive
analogy. The irony that develops to be a note of
consideration by subsequent authors, such as Soren
Kierkegaard, is found in the event that brings the
contradiction into view: Though Kant's argument
concludes that we cannot know a thing "in-itself"
except within or as a condition of knowledge,
nevertheless does reality seem to function upon this
contradiction in terms (an inherent and denied
absurdity). The issue since Kant is how the content of
the analogy, the 'fiction' of the analogy or meaning
of the discourse, breaks through the façade of its
facsimile to be able to be the content which then is
the actual thing that is Reason. This is one definition
of an ideal state, or what philosophy has deemed
Idealism, because the truth of the matter of all things
resides in the thought, Reason, or for a more honest
term, the Idea.

cleared up in philosophy, but in the end, merely passed over. However, it is the same problem that occurs with Kant; namely, are we talking about an Ideal issue, various situations that thinking sorts out, decides upon and in general, creates the whole of human existence? Or are we talking about a situation *wherein* thought finds itself. These are not only two argumentative points, but indeed indicate two distinct manners by which to even frame a discussion, to have an arena in which to discuss. Yet, philosophy, by nature of the assumed access that every human being has to it and ability to contribute to it, deals with these two situations, evidently and obviously, in the same manner, as they might be functioning in the same way, i.e. *as a concept.* Therefore and thereby what we are calling *philosophy* is not speaking of the situation that these blatantly different meanings indeed pose before us in a common area; thus we must make a distinction through this essay and categorize *conventional philosophy* as concerning what is common. This essay concerns this contradiction in method as well as what Event[37] might occur

---

[37] I make a distinction between a real event and the

for a *recognition* of the situation at hand, over a merely a thoughtful understanding of it.

*

This is the situation that Roland Barthes speaks about as the *pleasure* of the text[38]. To convey an even more particular and perhaps less ambiguous meaning, we might even say to the text, "at your pleasure", but then we might strike a nerve, at that, too soon. For all that has been written about this phenomenon, it is not a common occurrence. As we get into the body of this essay we will find Slavoj Zizek speaking about when a political actor becomes a revolutionary agent. He points out that it is not when the individual is involved in the act of blowing up a building, say, but afterwards when he (or others) begins to speak about the Event in a particular context. Rudolf Otto

---

Event, as this essay will elaborate, where the former is the condition for argument and the latter is the significance of traversing the field of reality, that is, *not real*. But for all true purposes, this distinction is a moot point due to the nature of the Event itself.

[38] Roland Barthes, "*The Pleasure of the Text*".

inadvertently describes to us the same thing when he tells us how religions are formed *around* an event[39]. The common manner of viewing the world is as an uninterrupted continuum of Being which can be chopped up and presented in a multitude of ways; the common manner normalizes events in to common occurrences (redundancy) so that, for instance, as Zizek tries to shed light upon the point, the emancipatory Event of the subject is always set aside and missed, or again, as Latour might say, *passed over*. What is common text, what is the common manner by which text is viewed, is thinking about all the various ways we might come upon text as a piece of writing: One way is pleasurable, another is pleasurable in one way[40]...But Derrida (as other authors also) is keen to consistently re-route this common manner of reading back toward what is *common of the text*, and what is common of the text is that there is no division in types, such as *this piece* of text is fiction, *this* piece is news, *this* piece is historical, oh, but *that* piece is nonsense. Seeing in every text what

---

[39] Rudolf Otto. "*The Idea of the Holy*".
[40] Other authors, Zizek included with Lacan, go into all the facets of the French *Jouissance.*

is common of the text, what is *common* though the encounter with text, is an *uncommon* manner of coming upon text. Text, in this way, is not localized unto script, or symbols, or books. Text is Derrida's way of discerning what is occurring *through* thinking, *as* thought. The common manner would particularize 'text' distinguished from 'thought' or 'activity' or 'doing'; but his point is that all these things are textual, all these things are *discursive*.

I submit that the terms of discourse are significant where the text has been normalized. Again; the operative statement here is, "If there is something outside of discourse, then what is it?" At every juncture of attempt to tell us something that is outside of discourse, discourse appears as the totality of existence; hence, the term stands in the place of that thing that is presumed outside of the text. The common view looks to the particular thing *that the text points to*; the uncommon view sees the text, or as has been said elsewhere, the terms[41]. This

---

[41] Lance Kair. "*The Moment of Decisive Significance*". The issue is the term.

recognized situation, the one of the description of the uncommon view of the one of the common and the uncommon, and the one that describes the contradiction inherent of this philosophical situation, is the Wittgenstein Collapse.

Anything else that is cognized is continuously upheld in a conventional transcendental suspension[42]. This is the main issue through all philosophy; i.e. the extension of the common beyond what we are calling the Wittgenstein Collapse.[43] This is to say that even as the common manner was indeed compromised it was and is still assumed as *the* common manner, and the meaning of the common manner is that everything and anything can be communicated in potential across a common category. Reality is this potential. What we find, though, is that the attempt to

---

[42] Note that I turn Kierkegaard's ideas on their head in order to have fidelity in this age with what he presents. His question actually concerns what is true in the context of this essay.
[43] This is nothing more than a rephrasing or recontextualization of Descartes's *thought* and *extension*, and then identifying with the extension for the ground of Being.

communicate what is uncommon to what is common has failed. This is what Derrida reads of Heidegger's "destitution of spirit"[44]; what once involved the potential of the common has been left destitute. What was common has become a surface of itself, as Zizek points out as well as Deleuze, an inversion of Platonic Ideal forms: The screen is the surface of sense around material body, the route of 'transcendental ideals' having been incapable of being sustained as spirit-in-itself[45].

The inversion is exactly what we have described above, where every moment becomes an event, a continuum of potential where every moment holds the possibility of an event, such that the subject of emancipation (the Event) loses its credibility as a viable reality because it has already been emancipated from the One reality of a common Ideal. The spirit, if before was indicated through methods of fulfillment, such as religion but also now modern humanist spirituality, now becomes

---

[44] Jacques Derrida. "*Of Spirit*".
[45] The point here is that in the (post-)modern context spirit precipitates out of suspension.

bankrupt, 'less than nothing', as Zizek's book of the same name describes what value spirit has in today's economy of real things: The event of spirituality has the same power for significance as any other real thing, ultimately reckoned by arbitrary subjective contingencies of meaning; like the individual of an audience that identifies with what is substantial through the media screen.

What is ideal for our conventional state, the thing that remains out of reach for the present material reality, is no longer in reference to some centralized ideological ethical-forms 'out-there' somewhere, but is directed from an idealized of material body of physical-empirical form 'in-here'. Modern methods of spirit, rather than rejecting the vulgar, physicality of the body, now see the body as the source of spiritual harmony. The shift can be understood as purely discursive[46]. This kind of *pass*, where the shift is not even recognized as a shift between like options, allows us to consider

---

[46] The shift has only a coincidence with real belief. As we will read below, belief concerns the term-object identity.

how existential modes function to maintain a particular state. Again, we have support for a linkage between philosophy and addiction.

Lyotard

discourse and communication

Technology draws us. Jean-Francois Lyotard's issue is communication. Being, discourse, and communication are the issues of the postmodern condition: What is Being, how does it manifest, and is this manifestation communicable?[47] The answer Lyotard gives us is the conditions under which the situation *should be able to be* communicated. He tells us that our relationship with technology has shifted such that now we speak of the legitimacy of Being through a discourse that is defined by experts. This difference (to de-*ffer*, e.g. to the experts) manifests due to technology being a *component* system of interacting parts (what I call 'objects'), while what is

---

[47] (L) We consider Lyotard's two main works, "*The Postmodern Condition*", and "*The Differend*". The former concerns the subject's relationship with technology, and the latter concerns the potential for communication.

not communicated through this scheme (what is left behind or left out) is not compensated for appropriately or with justice to the offense that has been committed in the attempt to coordinate the parts.

When we begin to understand the issue at hand within the history of Western Philosophy (as concerns ontology in general, and the continental vein in particular), the offense that has not been recompensed is the involvement of Being in *the failure of communication*. This is the notice that begins with Nietzsche and Kierkegaard but receives its final blow with Wittgenstein: Something is missing, or, something vital and significant is not being communicated. The (post-) modern[48] restitution for the failure of communication then arrives through identity, which is to say, through a simple denial of the failure itself through changing focus or frame. Identity, by

---

[48] The modern and the post-modern define the parameters of modern reality. Zizek frames this through a political term: Capitalism. And the two philosophical paradigms constitute the Marxist elaboration of modern human reality.

another term, thus becomes the cardinal feature of technological formation: Technology is the work of identification. Technology is the construction of tools from the assemblage of parts, and the person who knows how to make useful tools or knows how to use them well, is an expert. How the assembly occurs loses importance *because* of the failure of communication, so communication forms itself into a technology which does not consider (as a reframed definition) the failure of its knowing: Technology becomes the containment that is successful communication, the suspension whereby reality is inherent.

The condition through which the nature of Being should be able to be communicated is thus the proper understanding of the subject's relationship with technology. Yet, this is not a common understanding nor is it being communicated through conventional philosophy; hence the finding of the necessity to speak in a certain manner. We should note, then, that *discourse* is a technology. In fact, when we read about various localities of technology, the various kinds of technology, we should be able to discover in Lyotard's texts[49] that his use of those technological terms and their associated causal intensions (objects and how they are used) conveys a meaning that is not inconsistent with the discourse we have thus far entertained around Derrida and Deleuze. The terms of discourse and how they are used to establish Being give rise to two ontological bases, or what I call two orientations upon objects.

The particularizing of clauses to contextual localities must follow a necessary correspondence that resists isolation into *causal* lineage. Given a situation, only a certain set of responses may be offered for any occasion of discourse to make sense, but that each of these possible responses with reference to that sense extend to reduce the total possible response for any condition to one or infinity; either it is a specific cup as such, or it dissolves into a multiplicity of subjective meanings. In other words, what is understood as cause has already occurred

---

[49] That is, his two works above, (L), a *phrase universe* and the apparent failure of communication between phrase universes.

and is inherent to the presentation of technology, but it only functions that way under particular conditions which are not common[50], and in fact are not communicable as a set of instructions. The analogy of this incompatibility of ontological casual certitude is that we do not ask for the cause of the T.V./computer monitor that is giving me my nightly entertainment/social interaction, but indeed if we were to ask, the lines of causation would extend into such multiplicity of vectors as to become a meaningless query on one hand, and would yield an aggregate of investigation which would come up with arguments for what is actually the cause of that event, albeit, under certain conditions. There is no instructions for how to traverse the given of the TV/computer to the explanation for why or how it is the case. The traversal exists as a categorical imperative which cannot be communicated through, to or for, the One route.

---

[50] What is common is to overlay 'the' ontological truth of intensional subjective relativity upon the actual instance of instruction.

While a part may fit with a number of other parts, function limits which parts may be used and still have sense; the fact that we are able to assemble any parts together with any other parts does not mean that *everything* has *no* sense, or that it is all meaningless or based in nothing. On the contrary; the plasticity of any part with reference to function is itself a singular sensibility, a part that did indeed align only with particular parts which has sense for its exact functioning. Sense must have a particular meaning for there to be any sense at all[51]; the indication is not that it all means nothing or has no ground, rather, it just means that if sense can mean anything then there is no causal basis by which to have any causal lineage, because we inevitably are led then to ask what caused causation? And we know where that leads:

---

[51] A sensation removed from all meaning, such as the immediate sensation of a bee sting, has the meaning of having no sense in one moment, and then having a multiplicity of potential sense in another, including that is was a bee sting. The attempt to isolate what is meant by sense in thus a move into real causality which normalizes the event into modern ideological nothingness, in effect, passing over the nonsense of the sting itself.

To an ontological argument about the meta-physics of the One universe, a particular model of how sense is to be properly experienced to be real. The cause of this sense, then, cannot be determined from a logic of experience because of the nature of experience itself (redundancy).

Where have we heard of this situation before? It is the situation of Kant's *synthetical a priori* before the Collapse. It is the working ignorance of there being no reason why reason should give us any sense or any world at all. The *synthetic a priori* is the notice of this problem for which it supplies a conceptual structure out of nothing to explain and ground the contradiction: The redundancy arises as nothing (again) is proposed to supply the building blocks of something. So then after Wittgenstein we find the rift which brings The Two Routes: The determined Pure Reason and the contingent Practical or hypothetical Reason. Repetition is the coming upon the same problem again and again through different terms[52]; the terms of our moment is technology.

---

[52] Kant develops his philosophy around the notions of

The subsequent exploitation by the nervous 20th century clergy of 19th century Reason then is thwarted with a return to honesty and response at the beginning of this 21st century. Cause must be understood for what it actually presents to reason, which is to say that cause occurs vicariously, or through an other, *before* the miscue phenomenal reaction inspired by Kant. This is thus the first change that must occur, and it is at root a religious or ontological alteration in the approach of how work is to be accomplished. Before the collapse there was no ability to know *through* an other as we see evidenced by Hegel's synthetic world historical consciousness[53]. So once the synthetic unity

---

Pure and *Practical* reason, but as well *categorical* and *hypothetical* imperatives. These are two manners of speaking about the same situation. Kierkegaard then elaborates upon how the irony inherent in this division plays out for subjectivity.

[53] Hegel's common assumption that it is only through the phenomenal spirit of reason that things are known, the other is an operational mechanism of reason. Keep in mind that this is not necessarily a discounting of this phenomenal manner because in fact there is the real argumentative philosophical

of reason is fractured by "Being-there", or *Dasein*, the 'there' which by its nature is at once sure in its synthetical reason and yet ambiguous and full of disaster in its application, then we have a condition where we are not able to know for sure either way. The condition that Lyotard describes emerges to thus to be brought current *by virtue* of the other, as we call it now, the universal object.

*

A "phrase universe" is the term Lyotard uses to relate the situation of textual correspondence and relations that we encounter as the world. The use or extension of this context upon a category that is outside of its purview, namely, the world *to which* it is subject, manifests in a condition that he calls the "metanarrative". In his essay, he defines "postmodern as incredulity toward meta-narratives"[54]. The exception to this contingency –the

---

route that depends on *asserting* the null hypothesis as its operational mode. We find the notice for the requirement of religion in this sense.

[54] Lyotard. *"The Postmodern Condition"*.

coincidence of the metanarrative and the incredulity toward it – is thus determined by those who would be able to best use the technology necessarily; as above, that is the experts, and hence the injustice to Being is supposed to be recompensed by the workings of technology. Here we have another theoretical posture that gives and then takes back in one move, a solution to Being that is only solved in the formulation that has been made by the expert who understands the metanarrative and is incredulous toward it, which is to say the phrase universe asserting itself as 'The' universe[55].

Another way to view the situation is by replacing the term 'injustice' with 'misunderstanding'[56]. Lyotard's book *"The Differend"* uses an analogy of the court hearing to describe the situation of the postmodern condition of Being. He asks, how can a case be made to a court that

---

[55] The mode of the expert thus must be description over argument. This is the progressive move because description no longer detracts from that which is outside of its purview, by definition.

[56] And indeed, Jacques Lacan's 'mistake'.

cannot understand the case or does not recognize the evidence? How can justice be served? But, the issue is not that the courts merely misunderstand, but indeed that they cannot even hear the case –but that they hear it anyways. The picture that he draws is that the court does not admit it's ignorance, but instead behaves, indeed, sees the case that is brought as indeed the case that is presented, as of a common identity, and so offers restitution based upon the judgment made upon what knowledge it has gained through the hearing. It is the recompense ruled through this kind of hearing that Lyotard says amounts to an injustice. Hence the problem with the real affiliation of (post-) modern identity and Being.

The issue is communication and the condition through which communication should take place. What is meant by *should* is that indeed activity takes place around the notion or idea of communication, but that indeed we still are not quite sure exactly what is occurring[57]. But is

---

[57] This is similar to the topic of Heidegger's "*What is Called Thinking*", where what is most interesting or

communication taking place? What do we mean by communication? In the context of justice, that which is just is commensurate with the truth; hence, communication takes place when the truth has been communicated truthfully. But how are we to discern what this truth is, let alone if it is being communicated? Here we see the injustice; for, if we have to ask for the criterion by which such a communication may be sound, then we are asking into the surface 'sub-sistence' of the screen, that object of technology by which the proper tool manifests for the ability to discern truth, which is then by this reference 'not-truth', but rather an interlocutor through which what is true may likewise denote reality. We have now returned to the same problem situation we notice of Kant: How does what is asking of truth break through the surface of the fiction of the screen to encounter what is *actually* true[58]? By an act of redundancy. We can start to understand how conventional philosophy shows evidence of using logic as an instrument to

---

thought-provoking is that we have not yet begun to think.

[58] See note (k) on Kant.

instill and enforce dogma, rather than a tool to use for truth.

Prehistory: Wittgenstein and Badiou

We must speak in a particular manner if we are to get off the path and see what is truly there. The path has become the world, but everyone knows that such a world is not all there is; this is the dilemma before us. This manner of speaking must be particular to marking that which is not in reference to the path; it must set up an arrangement for the use of discourse under a new condition. Zizek, through Lacan, calls this condition a Master Signifier. In other words, while not being able to escape the known paths, we nevertheless speak as though no path exists yet known. Also, one of the reasons accompanying this essay shows that if we wish to talk about things that are not religious, that is, if we wish to heretical, then we can no longer recourse to irony; when we have to encounter what is real, we have to confront our faith.

*

A history of philosophical division has already been noted and established with the *analytical* and *continental* traditions; we can truly say in light of what is communicated by these traditions has largely failed. More precisely, if we wish to be honest, and not merely argumentative, then we must speak of the situation as having failed. If there is one important thing to gain from the reading of Wittgenstein's philosophy, it is that philosophy collapses at his moment, the moment that we are allowed to identify with him (an ideal construct, since he lived for 62 years). Nevertheless, in a quite real sense, there is nothing more to be said after that moment of identification with the situation presented by his work, for we have identified with something that cannot be identified: The manner of identification has collapsed and thus has to be intensionally, (which is to say with reference to what has gone before) artificially held up.

Yet, plenty more has been said and continues to be said. Notwithstanding the ridiculousness, this situation of this essay does not concern what defines the division of those philosophical traditions so much because, on one hand, Wittgenstein was in the Analytical school, his mentor Bertrand Russel, and his focus much to do with math and logic. On the other hand, it is possible to draw a straight line from him to Alain Badiou, who is of the supposed continental tradition; through his book *"Being and Event"*, Badiou proposes a way to unify the two schools.

Like a fold in space-time, when we notice what is occurring of these two philosophers, it can appear something has been missed[59]. The empty set that is come upon in Wittgenstein does not actually occur as an explainable phenomenon until Badiou moves to explain the opposite of collapse. Badiou's whole philosophy concerns the Event where what has shown itself as *nothing*, collapse, end with no beginning, that which yet continues to *Be*, continues in some manner. Apparently, we must find the Event that is the fact of Wittgenstein's at once *made no difference and made a difference*. If philosophy recognizes the significance of the *"Tractatus Logico-Philosophicus"*, the tiny book and the

---

[59] Again, the question of "can you see it?"

only book that Wittgenstein published in his lifetime, then there is a contradiction at work in the making of any comment upon it; in fact, we could say that since the *Tractatus*, philosophy itself has been in suspension, functioning without a theoretical license that recognizes a link between what is being said and what a world might be: Functioning through a negativity. Likewise, then, we find the significant problem: Philosophy does not behave as if it is occurring in this suspension. On the contrary, it behaves as if nothing significant has occurred, which is to say, as though Wittgenstein's book did not mean what it meant, and this is to say, that the meaning of his book is not what he meant but is indeed the meaning that has been put to use in a particular manner, and that 'significance' is just another term which perpetually evades its meaning for the definition, which is to say, for argument[60] . Strangely enough, we do hear reports that

---

[60] The difference: Either meaning informs definition, or definition allows for meaning. It's an example of a chicken-or-the-egg philosophical dilemma for which conventional philosophers can spend a career formulating a position.

this is exactly the situation that Ludwig himself said would occur.

*

This essay is not going to make an argument about what Wittgenstein really means either, nor what could be more true about his writings. Where I might proceed upon that endeavor, there I might be further evidencing the same fault that brings down the significance of the continental tradition. Difference *as* difference marks the condition, indeed, as has been discussed thoroughly elsewhere. Ironically, the fault is evident in as much as the *implied* description did not convey the necessary inherent truth of itself (in and for itself) but still evidenced something missing, what many authors have noted, in their various ways, as *excess*. This excess could be said to be represented as a distance which then disappears being traversed. For instance; involved with the above situation between Wittgenstein and Badiou, the traversal appears nothing less than the folding of space-time[61]. The situation to be

---

[61] We find a close coordination with Kierkegaard's

noticed is that there is no reduction to be made, and, the continental tradition is or has been the effort to reduce what is 'in essence' to what is, shall we say, 'not essence', what is material to what is empirical in some discourses, what is ideal to what is real in others, what is different to what is common in yet another. We can say with confidence that with the last reductions of Alain Badiou and François Laruelle, the continental case is, again, either closed, or still functioning in a suspension of meaning that has missed something[62]. Zizek tells us about a collapse of this kind of reckoning based upon distance; I take this to its end: No argument is to be made.

Instead, a description is to be put forth. This essay concerns what is perpetually missed in philosophy: If we are talking about ontology, if philosophers are

'contemporary' addressed in *Philosophical Crumbs.*
[62] A 'last reduction' is meant in the non-philosophical sense: An argument that either must admit of its own fault, that its entire method is incorrect, or change the rules of the game without acknowledging that a change has been made, that is, through denial or deception.

putting forth ontological arguments, arguments about what Being might actually be or what it *Is*, then how is there disagreement? Why are we still talking about it? In particular to this question, so often we come to this moment in philosophy through a feeling which then demands some sort of move; the idea does not just stand for itself, we *feel* compelled (reason does not compel us in this instance) as critical theorists to argue why it is needed as a concept by arguing how it can be applied to other concepts that further appear to be necessarily connected: Philosophy itself speaks to this grounding ubiquitous progress in knowledge. We see the course of history for philosophical ideas has been moving in a particular direction, mounting, if you will, along certain tensions and conceptual defaults to bring philosophy as a common venture to this inevitable juncture...Even here, in this First Part, such an ideal movement is suggested as it is relied upon in speaking about Wittgenstein... back then, having marked a moment of collapse, etc... but why should there be any debate as to why or why not this is true?

*

As stated earlier, this essay will deal with things that are inherently offensive to thought; we must speak in a particular manner. The goal is to destroy the transcendent, the *synthetical a priori*, not only theoretically, semantically or discursively, but indeed, *actually*[63]. Only in this move will we have a definite parameter by which to reckon what it is to be human, a parameter which will then give philosophy a ground by which to discern what is *actually occurring*. We then can speak of what consciousness is doing as Being, as universal inclusion that does not then work again to again distance itself from itself for the purpose of hiding its motivations in subjective agency. We will have a ground by which to speak of philosophy as a scientific venture.

---

[63] The teleological imperative of the Event is the destruction of the *synthetic a priori*.

Zizek and the Event: the occasion for discourse.

This essay is a hack into a particular philosophical manner that holds one of its attributes as sacrosanct. Conventional philosophy operates within a limit which is commonly defined as infinite and non-existent; so thorough is this understanding of infinity that it cannot be spoken about without a corresponding referral to something else within the limit. We can call this the phenomenon of philosophy, but a better term has been coined: Correlationalism[64] is simply an inability to admit limit, and I have termed the effort which continues through this limit as *conventional philosophy*. This effort must then be said to have definition: Due to the ubiquity and omnipresence of subject matter (matter which subjectivity is concerned with) that conventional philosophy presents to its users (the method is self-reflecting, self-evident), it is

[64] Quentin Meillassoux. "*After Finitude*".

incapable of presenting a view to the limit inherent of its operation. In accordance to the axiom of this method (of limit, which is an essential and functioning limit and not just a defined limit) the object to which the term "correlationalism" might refer (which is actually philosophy itself) is displaced so philosophy does not have to be concerned with indicting its own method for the assertion of proper Being; the method is effectively equivalent to an implicit ontological argument and thus proposes as it defends axiomatically the only kind of Being that is *allowed* to exist. As I have said, the conventional philosophical method is redundant, but it also operates through the *pass*, which is a theoretically polite manner of saying *denial*.

One of the founding rebuttals of philosophy asks "...but what do you mean by *x*?" This is *the* mode of operation by which conventional philosophy can disclaim any proposal, and, as well, the method by which it claims access to every situation that exists, that which allows access to every possibility in potential[65]. It is also the

---

[65] Subjectivity lays claim to the creation of whole

reason why we have the correlational conundrum of *nihilism*: Because, coincidentally, if we ask into every statement, and further in to every term, the result is the Wittgenstein Collapse which places us in a universe suspended in nothing, swirling in endless reference to infinite relativity, using a discourse that is grounded in nothing[66]. The conclusion, the

worlds; the free agent lays claim to do anything within its desire; transcendence is the way one is able to know anything at all. Immanence is just another way of claiming a communication with aspects which are outside of reality. This is to say, knowledge of reality is a transcendental operation.

[66] The opposite of the Collapse is also Hegel's World Historical Consciousness, the 'fullness' of Reason. But they are two ways to speak about the same thing. Hegel's is the culmination (synthesis; might we say *fusion?*) which occurs when asking and finding no answer to 'the last question'; there is nothing left but to 'jump' from the conclusion like Kierkegaard (continental subjectivity). Wittgenstein is the Collapse (can we say *fission?*) which occurs likewise when there is no answer to be found – nothing for an answer – that the only answer is to throw away the whole game (analytical objectivity). Strangely enough, using the analogies of physics: Both unleash vast amounts of (creative) energy. Badiou speaks to the unspeakable (thus unknown, void) which allows

solution to this conclusion, as Jean Paul Sartre tells us, is to 'revolt' from the abyss, and, in short, manipulate discourse to establish our real identities. In other words, if there is no actual ground, then we are free to choose our own ground, our destinies.

So, to back pedal a little; the conventional route uses this method to get out of what is correlational of Being: It simply sees what is 'correlational' as having no essential ground but the discourse which is used to found it, and side-steps the issue by placing what is correlational into a definition outside of which is nothing but the discourse that we are then allowed to manipulate to establish a new identity.

the term-object identity

I refer to the criterion by which this infinite possibility is available to thought, the mechanism of intensional suspension, as the *term-object identity*. The term-object identity founds the One Route, or what we can call the orientation upon

---

for these kinds of processes.

True Objects. The onto-theological equation for the common Reality goes like this: Thought is able to generate novel conceptions and ideas based upon a consideration of objects that have an essence that is effectively different than that of the thinker. Thought generates such novel ideas spontaneously, according this ability to communing or otherwise interacting with an unknown source, or a source which cannot be definitively proven, but is nevertheless relied upon. This source is spoken about in many ways, each with their various arguments and proofs; God, subject, brain/body, void, etcetera; this essay tends to use the term 'consciousness' to speak about it, though this is but a transitional term[67]. This phenomenon is so present and elusive that it can be said to encompass an ability to function through any configuration of sense or cognitive sensibility. These sensibilities are as numerous –and indeed more numerous –as they are debated. Without placing judgment upon the veracity of the titles, we can name a few which appear as 'far' from each other,

---

[67] One could say that *consciousness* is the founding term of this essay.

as each is able to 'prove' the falsity of the others without any room for error. Science; magic; philosophy; Christianity; Buddhism; Islam; atheism; Scientology; capitalism; monarchy; communism; Paganism; superstition; democratic; phenomenalism; idealism; republican; psychology; realism; neuroscientist; economics; citizen; human rights; apartheid; musician; humanism; artist; post-humanism; astrophysics; Wicca; philosophy; to name only a small fraction that appear on the immediate Western scene. Such sensibilities can overlap, and a person can use any number of these titles to identify oneself and what they think, as well, to establish sites for critique.

Despite how each might be able to be noticed to function within the limitation inherent to the title, which is to say, as identities each with a corresponding voice, they, as a category, nevertheless are able to show how *consciousness* functions[68] regardless of whether or not they are able to present any proof for why they may represent any truth in any moment. For instance, the scientist may not be able to

---

[68] Operates or does work.

view the world as functioning through Paganism though the former might have a way to explain the pagan scientifically, and each may present their objections of the other with proofs that are self-evident to themselves, but then show the 'proof' of the other's fallacy to that other. The Pagan may say, here is proof of Bumba's work, but the scientist will talk about potential and kinetic energy; the Pagan will then perhaps say those are aspects of Bumba's power, and the Scientist will maybe mention psychological terms; the debate will go on and on and perhaps escalate until one side gives up, or they decide to agree to disagree.

This happens everywhere, even within frames that would suppose they agree as to the frame; this occurs so often, that I doubt I need give examples. Yet further, even as we might be able to establish this general category, there is no obvious arguable proof that I could give as to why this category might be functioning any differently than the ones that are *of* the category. This is the principle of correlationalism in action, constantly rerouting all discourse back into the discursive horizon as though discourse is filtering through a grounding principle (what we philosophers often called Logic). This principle thus gives a 'The' ground upon which all things exist. This is to say that Logic is elevated to a kind of 'meta-discursive' essence, co-habitating with Reason which then is, for lack of a better term, an essential universal tool which exists effectively outside of the universe while nevertheless breaching the firmament to bestow upon human beings the ability to discern actual truths of existence. I would argue logic, when coupled with a particular method (that we can call practical, hypothetical, or conventional philosophy), then appears as an object of *faith*.

*

Against this real relativity within which all things reside we can most surely find a correspondence with Wittgenstein's Collapse, but searching for a way out of the correlation we might wish to consult Alain Badiou's *"Being and Event"* for a very good argument concerning a set that can be said to not be included in another set. For the purposes of this essay we simply resort to what seems sensible: A statement that has the most explanatory power can be said to be *true*. The ability or activity of discourse to relate to every other term of its economy, rather than only one or some terms, can be said to be a true assessment, but it only holds a greatest explanatory power to the extent that we see it *as indicating something more than* itself, which then by the assertion that discourse does not refer to anything outside of itself, contradicts that discourse can be manipulated or is giving us all there is through negotiation. To ask if there is anything outside of discourse is not an epistemological question here as much as it is a *logistical* question. Philosophy is not *always* about metaphysics and ontology; what is even more challenging and confronting in its nature is *truth* and *teleology*.

being and identity

The dividing of humanity and Being into multi-vocalities, a concept which delves into every micro-corner of identity as an attempt to establish a legitimacy of presence, is no longer truly significant. Yet, as Zizek illustrates with the Warner Brothers Roadrunner and Coyote cartoon[69], announcments only speak about what is occurring and frame it to awareness; the Coyote still needs the time to look down, see that he is standing on air and wave "bye", before he actually falls. In the philosophical-critical end, when identity dissolves itself into a theoretical multiplicity so thin as to threaten coherency, we are left with a group of isolated and alienated individuals, all of which view themselves in the context of a *nothingness* which often translates into an expressed psychological meaning as 'no one else understands'; as a basis of identity, a substance which must be gained solely through assertion is exceedingly difficult to give up. As well then, the strategy of manipulation and dishonesty that proceeds from alienation makes it even more difficult to have a discussion; for, how else is

---

[69] The famous scene (which happens in many cartoons in many ways) is when the Coyote is chasing the Roadrunner and the Roadrunner runs off a cliff. The one that comes to mind is that the Coyote runs into the cloud of thick dust kicked up in the Roadrunner's wake and he does not see that he has followed to Roadrunner off a cliff into thin air. At some point, the Coyote stops next to the Roadrunner, ready to get him, until he realizes something odd: there is no ground beneath them. He then falls.

someone so alienated supposed to get heard? Such a methodology works as a template by or through which work may be accomplished –we do what we need to in order to get the job done –but as a description of what the human being *is,* what *any* Being is, it is faulty. The current real template for Being thereby prescribes as it mandates a reciprocated dishonesty of subjectivity, a redundancy, a state that argues itself, as though we are naturally this way, alienated from the world and each other, alone in a hostile world. This may have been the case, or at least a sensible manner of operating in the world while we were still subjected to its mysteries, but the only mystery we have now is how much more abuse our world can take.

The 20th century can be seen as evidence of growing pains, of humanity, as an ideal category, attempting to assert this alienation upon the object of our woe in a last-ditch effort to prove to ourselves we are right in this 'natural' manner of being human, to 'make true' through joining what is immanent (alienated) with what is 'real'[70]

---

[70] Much of 20th century philosophy can be understood

. Further, perhaps we can notice how German Idealism, and indeed Enlightenment thinking in general, were (are) misunderstood as misapplied. From here then we might catch a glimpse of how and why Hitler and the Nationalist Socialists could have been so philosophically situated and determined, as well as how Heidegger could have appeared to be so ethically flexible[71]. Both exhibit the same psychology of the subject of an anxiety disorder attempting to placate his discomfort through eliminating or subjugating the perceived object of stress, that object which re-presents the problem inherent to the 'enlightened mind'[72]; one

---

as the effort to map what is alienated onto a real platform. This is nothing less than what went before in the historical attempt to impose (transcendental) righteousness: The immanence of subjectivity attempting to reconcile knowledge (of itself) with something that (apparently) is different from itself, but proposing in this that thus reality itself is indeed subjectively manifested, or otherwise negotiated by extension, with other subjectivities.

[71] Martin Heidegger joined the Nazi Party in 1933 by choice.

[72] The 'enlightened mind' is used here not in a qualitative sense; it is not the 'enlightened awareness'

though demand, the other through patronage and submission: The oppressing world[73]. Georg Hegel, Sigmund Freud, Jacques Lacan and Zizek grant us this *natural* model of that state which is no longer necessary; Zizek, always and in the last, granting us the view of the problem and thus its solution by showing us the limit of the subjective nature that was given for the others.

*

First, though, Kierkegaard and Nietzsche show us what the solution looks like *from* this natural state: *The absurdity of nothing* brought them angst and despair; both consumed by the truth of their view and the frustration of not being able to get anyone to see it, seeing it themselves but not being able to properly formulate into a commonly understandable discourse, shows in their work[74]. An alignment of what is

---

that is problematic. Rather, the problem is more the assumption that such an awareness should necessarily translate into a proper true world.

[73] The operative questions here are: What is oppression? What is doing the oppressing?

[74] A main tenant of Kierkegaard's work is what he

true with the argument of what *should be* true, demands one have no ground of Being except the avenue that goes between them by which to base activity; the

---

calls "*absurd*". The meaning of this term is a rejection of the ideological and religious abstractions that command regular daily life of the group (the crowd; the congregation), what he associates and conflates as "the ethical is the universal". In light of the ubiquity of such real abstractions, what is *absurd* is having something available to the subject that is *not abstract*, not 'surmised' from a set of intellectualized considerations, but rather something that is immediate, that is, beyond the mediation of the religious congregant, something that occurs outside of relation. The problem here, as it is always, is how such an immediate situation can be communicated to a situation that is mediated? Through every possible means that is available, it cannot, that is, except through an abstraction. The persistent attempt to communicate what cannot be communicated forms the ground of both Nietzsche and Kierkegaard's discourses, as well as the source of their respective intensities; namely, Nietzsche posits the "over-man", and Kierkegaard posits the "true-Christian", mythological characters that arise in each their own defensive postures as what *should naturally occur* given the present state of humanity. It is not difficult then to describe some of the outstanding events of the subsequent century in this light.

communication of the content of such a route being taken sounds, at best, absurd and nonsensical. Being becomes that isolated path[75], of *empty intension.*

Then, in this light, Heidegger's "tool use" takes on a whole new meaning. It does not reflect, by polemical inference of "a user" any sure core of "being-there" of anyone more than any other argumentative assertion. In fact, that nature of the tool in-and-for itself *must* withdraw from view – it must because it has something to hide[76]. As

---

[75] Alienation only come in play within an encompassing universe; isolation occurs when the alienation has been normalized.

[76] Graham Harman's *Object Oriented Ontology* is based much upon Heidegger's tool that withdraws from view. Harman's is merely another discussion about the situation of the *same* that Heidegger talks about, but under different terms. The same elements are able to be understood being reflected in different terms when we see that the elements are *present* and *given.* This is oppositional to the method that has argued that we create our own realities from the use of discourse. The *tool*, in the oppositional understanding, is not understood as an *empirical neutral* object as opposed to a *thinking and acting* subject; the tool in this instance is that which is/Being. This is the significance of O.O.O.: It places

a basis for understanding the human Being, political identity is an incorrect theoretical assertion appropriated by those who are unable know any better: In one state it is natural, in another it is ideological dogma. Political identity may be a means for human beings to get along in the world, but as a basis of the human Being, it is at best

all universal Beings on the same existential plane and does not privilege the central phenomenal thinker. In this model, that which creates its own reality must withdraw from view because the truth is that it is not creating anything. While the talking about the relations between objects is a useful manner to get things done, it does not reflect (or it only reflects) the Being that is being established through the use of the tool (technology; discourse). As we have said: a giving and a taking away. Nothing can get done in such a mode; we cannot take away what is given because we must have *something* to work with. This is redundancy in the act of being negated by irony, and the solution to this contradiction is: We must *only give* and the then *given* must be the totality of reality such that what *is*, Being, must withdraw; that is to say, in this methodology of focus upon what is *given* (conventional philosophy), that which *gives* is *not real*. Once this occupies reasonable knowledge, then what is not real in this regard, the (once subject, but now) object no longer withdraws to stay out of view, but is indeed what is leftover: Reality.

problematic. Is this not a true synopsis of the situation?

Hence, in order to shift the momentum we need keep in mind, though, some qualifications: A discussion of truth must include all the facts, or be able to account for the most facts of available proposals; such a statement cannot disregard facts out of hand; because often enough, just what the facts are or what constitutes a fact is arguable, the statement must account for a fact in a manner that is most explanatory for what a fact is; the explanatory power must affect the understanding in a manner that cannot be denied (or where only denial will work). This last criterion is the most ambiguous and so it will probably receive the most philosophical flack for it, but the meaning of it is an example of the factual nature of facts: We may feel that we want to explain them away, and indeed may have a certain sense of satisfaction in the argument we make as to the ambiguity of facts, but this activity does not necessarily invalidate that the fact is true. On the contrary, often enough it just means that we are able to constitute our 'world' in whatever way we see fit, regardless of the repercussions, just so long as it accommodates our reason-justified anxieties.

A very good example of this is a memory of a behavior we would like to have forgotten. Many times as we go on in our way, we find ourselves facing the occasion where we have to account for our behavior and we alter the truth. Sometimes we simply do not remember the truth of it; other times, perhaps, we outright fabricate reasons why the event occurred and why we responded the way we did. Regardless of the reason, if we are honest with ourselves, often we find that we are only forcing an interpretation that we attempt to justify to ourselves through telling others. As we will see further on in this essay, this kind of occurrence demands an explanation both for how it manifests *in* reality but likewise how it manifests *as* reality.

Philosophy holds a special place for such psychological aspects of theory: It argues away subjectivity into asserted argument; this is what subjectivity is: It is traditionally not an object of philosophy, but rather is the subject of philosophy. Perhaps this is why Zizek has said he is not a philosopher as much a social critic –because he has to exhibit what is contrary to what has been normalized for philosophy in order to speak truly of the situation at hand: He is concerned with the *subject of psychoanalysis*, which is really a kind of philosophical social-scientific object. Philosophy, rather, what we are calling conventional philosophy, likes to hold itself above opinion unless an argument reaches a stalemate; only then is the conventional philosophical object of worship, "Reason", allowed to admit any *personal* bias[77]. Emotional reaction is axiomatically excluded from Reason as a 'lesser' source of knowledge. Having a bad day does not play into philosophical reason, nor having someone destroy your prize proposal, nor hope for recognition and scholarly achievement. Conventional philosophy measures the argument only upon the credentials of use of its method[78], which

----

[77] Conventional philosophy understands its method as an *objective* method which is applied to the *subject*. Psychoanalysis –what I will refer to later as the Zizek-Lacan-Hegel platform – on the other hand, can be understood as a *subjective* method which is applied to the *object*, which is to say, *of philosophy.*

then shows us the redundancy instilled in its view. What it does not recognize is that an argument may have methodological order and sense and still not reflect the truth of the matter[79]. Are we able to find a

---

[78] Of course I am indicating its ideal. Conventional philosophy and its method is heavily weighted upon who you know – but this is also part of the method.

[79] We mean to indict the *Continental* school; it brings up complications by its own arrival on the scene, complications that find its presence an aggravating, rather than conciliatory aspect. By its very nature, it creates the condition where by things may not settle – which may, after all, be the point. Of course this is not to say that the Analytical school solves all problems, but the Analytical without question views Logic as synonymous to the method which avoids subjective ambiguity. Logic is a manner to have clear situations, questions and answers, as it does not rely upon subjective opinion as to why a result might occur. In this way, the Continental school can be seen to propose questions that arrive from nowhere definite, and give us answers that grant us little certitude.

I am nonetheless posing this from what many would consider a Continental Philosophical approach; I am also suggesting that there is no sure logical or scientific method, as a method, that is immune from subjective temperament. Both the Continental and Analytical approaches appear to rely

reason why the 'philosophically reasonable' method would want to argue that its method achieves results that must be the truth[80], why the argument is what matters, and has even gone so far as to say the results of the argument (discourse) *manifest reality*? Through these reasonable questions we might now be able to consider the problems we face with democratic capitalism, and why, as Zizek has suggested, it is so difficult to even *imagine*

---

upon, what is viewed by both in their respective a manners, a transcendent operation which allows human beings to avoid their own reflection and attitudes in the carrying out of the operations. Indeed, though, we can build great things and still have our subjective opinions based in nothing but bad attitudes. The issue I am pointing out here is that the Continental school lacks where it has come to see itself as digging up and erecting sure real things that are similar to houses or hospitals, or even the knowledge and skill by which a heart may be transplanted from a dead person into one that is living, at that, to give the latter a better quality of life. I am not sure what we have from the Continental school that gives us those kinds of things, as much as it might argue by its approach that it does.

[80] Even with the argumentative disclaimer: Such a disclaimer is a proposal of a true method for deriving truth.

outside of the capitalistic state. With this logic we are allowed then to consider the role *denial* plays in our current situation; it is not very difficult to get out of the capitalistic state, what is difficult is wanting to get out of it. Zizek's book *"Event"* is able to be understood as describing the Event that is not returned[81] to the common

---

[81] The issue to be filled out by this essay is about this "eternal return". Is anything being returned? If so, what is being returned? What does it mean that nothing is returned?

The question has been taken up, implicitly if not openly, by Alain Badiou and Francois Laruelle. Both of these authors grapple with the Postmodern issue of discrepancy and communication, but then apply solutions as to the maxim of no communication taking place. What is being communicated in this condition and of this condition has been solved by Badiou by claiming a kind of radical ontological rupture, an 'eruption' of the Void into the multiple which "begins the count" of real value. He suggests that the operator of truth, in the effort of truth, relinquishes such truth for the sake of the multiple, and that *this* is the radical condition of subjectivity which maintains fidelity. Laruelle, on the other hand, maintains the maxim of no communication. The condition of fidelity is the radical subjectivity *qua* subject (the subject as subject, and not subject as a condition of anything else, or as able to be

manner by which every moment contains an event in potential, where every philosophical argument must withhold something in an inherent interpretive ironic state, an Event that is indeed significant in its not returning.

The *term-object identity* is at the root of what we have called the One Route upon the world. Though this mechanism we are able to have objects; the term is understood to reflect, at least in part, the object of its reference. Whether the term actually reflects part of the object in

---

accommodated by anything else) is a unilateral condition which comes about through division, duality, but that this true state is not communicated across a boundary.

In distinction to these more polemical solutions, Zizek represents the situation where the condition itself cannot be extricated from any knowable situation except *as* the situation which is available to knowledge for any time, within knowledge as its own condition. In this way, he represents a position that never negates any other position, but behaves with 'equidistance' from each side; at once, occupying a radical intervention such as Badiou's, as well as a unilateral position that cannot be approached from any 'mistaken' understanding.

question is a moot point because we come upon the term as though it indeed is giving us the object to access and or act upon; it does not give as *an* object, the term gives us *the* object that we then work with. As much as we might be in a real situation, this identity grants us what is true, so we call such real objects *True Objects*, because they do not behave for us in reality as if they are merely a multitude of occasional, intangible, ideal facets of data.

A return from an Event back into the source of the Event is an act of redundancy. This act is based in the automatic recourse to what is understood as substantial. The Event itself is not substantial here; the event must have a substance to have meaning because the Event is automatically understood to have no content in-itself, its content is understood as real context and context is the multiplicity of events that constrained the Event to occur; the meaning of the Event is to coax out or otherwise look to the surrounding events, whether they be of the past, present or future. The term for this route, the function that is at root of this way to view events is the *term-object identity* because the thinking subject looks to the objects through their referent terms to gain an identity for what the event meant.

In this way, *every* object is an event in potential, because every object or situation that is presented can be viewed through this manner, what we call the *real* manner, *or reality*. If every situation that is presented to the thinking subject holds within itself a potential for an event, and the meaning of the event is found in the situation in which the event arises – this is redundancy by definition. Yet, the way, or mode that the phenomenal subject, the individual, comes upon reality is not through these theoretical tropes; people do not perpetually address every situation through the context of contextual elaboration. On the contrary; people see events as singular occurrences that reference various aspects depending on the very real context of what is available at the time, and there is a multiplicity, an infinite, an eternity of available contexts. Just think of how many books of fiction have been written; that is only a miniscule number of contexts in which an event may arise in their explanations.

We seem to have thus a contradiction between the theory and the lived experience of theory. To say that the theory is 'actually' describing the situation of the event, or is describing the actuality of the event, is a metaphysical speculation; it changes from day to day along the fashions of interest and indeed individual access to theory. The metaphysical idea is not as significant as the apparent discrepancy between the idea (which changes all the time and could be said to be merely another common event), and the actual occurrences where a person looks for an explanation of an event. The significant question is thus how these two circumstances reconcile? For how could I be even mentioning them if they have not reconciled somehow to experience? We thus will also address the notion of *conventional faith*, and how it is faith which allows for the impossibility of reality to coalesce.

The following essay is less a metaphysical discussion about ontology or Being. Rather, it is a hack into the ideological religious presence of philosophy itself. The following will be a truthful discussion about teleology and motion.

Bibliography

Badiou, A. (2005). *Being and Event.* (O. Feltham, & translation, Eds.) Continuum.

Barthes, R. (1975). *The Pleasure of the Text.* (R. Miller, & translation, Eds.) Hill and Wang.

Derrida, J. (1976). *Of Grammatology.* (G. C. Spivak, & translation, Eds.) The Johns Hopskins University Press.

Derrida, J. (1989). *Of Spirit.* (G. Bennington, R. Bowlby, & translation, Eds.) The University of Chicago Press.

Harman, G. (2002). *Tool Being.* Open Court.

Harman, G. (2007). *Heigegger Explained.* Open Court.

Harman, G. (2007). On Vicarious Causation. *Collapse*, 171-205.

Heidegger, M. (1968). *What is Called Thinking.* (J. G. Gray, & translation, Eds.) Harper & Row Publishers, Inc.

Heidegger, M. (1977). *Basic Writings.* (D. F. Krell, Ed.) Harper & Row, Publishers, Inc.

Kair, L. A. (2016). *The Moment of Decisive Significance: A Hersey.* Lance A. Kair.

Kant, E. (1998). *The Cirtique of Pure Reason.*
(P. Guyer, & A. W. Wood, Eds.)
Cambridge University Press.

Kant, E. (2004). *Prolegomena to Any Furture Metaphysics.* (G. Hatfield, Ed.)
Cambridge University Press.

Kierkegaard, S. (2009). *Repetition and Philosophical Crumbs.* (M. G. Piety, & translation, Eds.) Oxford University Press.

Land, N. (2012). *Fanged Noumena.* (R. Mackay, & R. Brassier, Eds.) Urbanomic.

Laruelle, F. (2013). *Principles of Non-Philosophy.* (N. Rubczak, A. P. Smith, & translation, Eds.) Bloomsbury.

Latour, B. (2013). *An Inquiry into Modes of Existence: An Anthropology of the Moderns.* (C. Porter, & translation, Eds.) Harvard University Press.

Lyotard, J.-F. (1984). *The Postmodern Condition.* Manchester.

Lyotard, J.-F. (1988). *The Differend.* (G. Van Den Abbeele, & translation, Eds.) University of Minnesota Press.

Meillassoux, Q. (2008). *After Finitude.* Bloomsbury.

Ortega y Gasset, J. (1960). *What is Philosophy.* W.W. Norton and Company.

Otto, R. (1923). *The Idea of the Holy.* (J. W. Harvey, & translation, Eds.) Oxford University Press.

Robinson, K. (2016, May 27). *Poem Guide. Robert Frost: The Road Not Taken.* Retrieved December 16, 2018, from Poetry Foundation: https://www.poetryfoundation.org/articl es/89511/robert-frost-the-road-not-taken

Wittgenstein, L. (1999). *Tractatus Logico-Philosophicus.* (C. K. Ogden, & translation, Eds.) Dover.

www.ingramcontent.com/pod-product-compliance
Lightning Source LLC
Chambersburg PA
CBHW060301050426
42448CB00009B/1708